I Shall Not Be Moved

Racial Separation
in Christian Worship

Terriel R. Byrd

UNIVERSITY PRESS OF AMERICA,® INC.
Lanham • Boulder • New York • Toronto • Plymouth, UK

Copyright © 2007 by
University Press of America,® Inc.
4501 Forbes Boulevard
Suite 200
Lanham, Maryland 20706
UPA Acquisitions Department (301) 459-3366

Estover Road
Plymouth PL6 7PY
United Kingdom

Library of Congress Control Number: 2007921277
ISBN-13: 978-0-7618-3715-2 (paperback : alk. paper)
ISBN-10: 0-7618-3715-9 (paperback : alk. paper)

Contents

Introduction

".. . We don't deal with this race issue, and we don't preach enough about it. I believe God is disturbed and hurt by that" (Bernice King).[1]

"I have a dream." These four words of Dr. Martin Luther King, Jr. are immortal. They express in poetic elegance the hopes and aspirations of people, around the world; those who love and yearn for freedom and justice. Perhaps no individual more conveyed, in sacrifice and service, the spirit and meaning of these words than did Dr. Martin Luther King, Jr.

I remind myself of several lines in the "I Have a Dream" speech that are not quoted as often as some others, but reflect the poignancy of Dr. King's message. He said,

> ".. . we will be able to speed up the day when all of God's Children—black men and white men, Jews and Gentiles, Catholics and Protestants—will be able to join hands and to sing in the words of the old Negro spiritual, "free at last, free at last; thank God Almighty we are free at last."[2]

I was only seven years old when Dr. King delivered what has now been labeled, in prose and form, one of the world's most famous speeches. At the time, in spite of my youth and lack of understanding of the substance of the Civil Rights Movement, I was nonetheless impressed by the sounds of its progress, all quite embodied in the words spoken by Dr. King. Even then, I understood the syntactical passion of Dr. King. I knew that he was extremely gifted. I knew that the articulate import of his words was mighty.

Now, more than four decades later, the speech still resonates with me, and around the world with meaning and hope, for all people who still want, love or seek justice and peace.

Dr. King voiced concerns about fairness in life everywhere and in all social institutions. He cared about the existence of right standing in practices in every sphere of American life. As much as this society at large was fragmented by racial injustice, he saw "The Church" equally as fragmented and stagnant, unable and unwilling to rise to its true moral responsibility on the serious issues of racism and segregation. Consequently, it was such that when Dr. King needed the full cooperation of the Church in America the most, it was not there for him.

Today, I take this opportunity to revisit the state of "The Church" to see whether it has grown or changed course on these two issues; to see how far it has come in the half-century since the height of Dr. King's struggle to bring racial equality to the heart of the nation, and to the Church in America. I want to look into it, too see if the Church is still a place that may well be empty and stagnant because it remains, in essence, separate at the core on matters of race.

Throughout the years of America's most serious moral and spiritual failure, the Church was not unified. For a generation, and rightly so, the bailiwick of Civil Rights was the spearhead of the so-called "Black Church." Though there were notable exceptions; by and large, mainstream Christianity ignored the plight of millions of black Americans who suffered second class citizenship, and systematic denial of their civil rights, in every sector of American life.

In this work, I seek to validate my own misunderstanding of the message of the gospel as it pertains to a whole and unified Church, and how Dr. King's message of peace, unity and hope dovetails with that of the Gospel, the preaching and the living of it. What is more, I wonder whether I can fully apply Dr. King's message of integration, of transcendence of artificial social barriers, to the spiritual arena—to the place he loved with all his heart, mind, body and soul—that is, to the Christian church.

It is a fact that in times of national tragedy, Americans unite immediately. On September 11, 2001, for example, Americans of all racial, ethnic, social and economic backgrounds came together as "one nation indivisible," to join forces to rescue the injured, to shore up the lives of the ones most deeply affected, to put out the flames from that ghastly and violent terrorist attack on our nation.

We all know that September 11, 2001 was a special occasion of unity in America. People from all walks of life merged, we had to, in order to appropriately comfort the hurting and the helpless. For people in New York City and Washington, D.C. who had their loved ones torn away from them by this senseless act of barbarism, Americans became one family, one fabric of human life and compassion, as the smoke consumed what was familiar and dear to all of us; as fires from the Twin Towers raged before our eyes and snatched life, as we knew it, and loved ones, away forever.

In Washington, our political leaders joined hands on the steps of the capitol and sang *God Bless America*. National prayer gatherings were observed throughout our country that transcended racial and ethnic lines. In this time of trouble, when our peace, and our way of life was threatened like never before, Americans joined their hearts as one. Yes, regardless of our religious, political, social and cultural differences, our nation came together. These common acts of unity and identity depicted who Americans are and proved that it is possible for this nation to unite around a single vision of hope.

Unfortunately, the tragedy of September 11 was another example of the catastrophic failure of religion, and of the human spirit—of the harrowing outcome of simplistic choices established and sanctioned by a narrow religious view. Still, that massacre of three thousands human souls provides evidence that King's prophetic voice points beyond the political to the religious and spiritual climate of our society. If religion does not and cannot transform people, improve the human condition, tame the human will at riot with itself, then what is its real mission?

Despite the plethora of issues that divide us in America—race, class, and values that relate specifically to race and class—the one question that presses most on my mind regarding our nation these forty years after the Civil Rights Movement of the 1950's and 1960's is: can and should King's call for desegregation, equality and unity, still concern and challenge the actions and formation of identity surrounding the Christian church in American society? In King's fight for equality, he observed and said, "Eleven o' clock Sunday morning is still America's most segregated hour, and the Sunday school is most segregated school of the week."[3]

Because the work of Dr. King made such a sea change in the outlook of the American social landscape, I was educated in an integrated public school system. My college and seminary experiences were integrated. Every secular job I ever held was in an integrated environment. Yet, my earliest religious experiences were all segregated. That's the way the church in America was and continues to be stratified. How bizarre it seemed to me that the church was the only social institution in which I was involved that remained, essentially, segregated along racial lines long after the gains of the Civil Rights Movement for social unity and equality.

As an ordained minister, I have long been as troubled and as perplexed by the inaction of the church, black and white, as was Dr. King, and by the assurances provided to it by the status quo of mandatory separateness of certain aspects of American life—especially by the sustained separate nature of church life; by the spiritual mandate in America of a separate, a segregated Church. Because the views and symmetry of separation have a special dynamic, if not a peculiar pathology, which needs to be examined by the faithful, I wonder why the Church in all its ethnicity, is at peace with itself.

I grew up in Ohio during the 1960's and 1970's in a black Baptist tradition in a small semi-rural community of approximately 16,000 people. Of course, all the neighborhood churches were divided, first along denominational lines, by color. Since these demarcations were so customary, I never perceived them to be the result of any intentional meanness or hatefulness from either the white or black religious institutions. I suspect that, in that era, most of the religious communities in town felt the same way: this is just the way things are, don't rock the boat!

So, in my town, we had the white Methodist church. And just two or three blocks away, there was the black Methodist church. Both congregations sang traditional Wesleyan hymns that united in the same melodic reframes. Also, there was the black Baptist church. Just two or three blocks away, there was the white Baptist church. Both congregations followed the same traditional pattern of extending invitations or calls to discipleship while often singing Billy Graham's favorite traditional hymn, Just as I Am. "Just as I am with out one plea, But that Thy blood was shed for me, And that Thou bidd'st me come to thee, O Lamb of God! I come! I come!"[4] (But with only those who look and act just like me!) Then, there was the Christian church (Disciples of Christ), one white and the other black. Both congregations followed their ritual of serving communion every Sunday. And there were the white Pentecostals and the black Pentecostals, both felt the Presence of the Spirit and expressed their awareness of that contact with ecstasy. They moved, they clapped their hands, and sang in robust vocal celebration of their great, good God. But they did it separately, in buildings that were located two miles apart.

It perplexed me that those Christian groups, which were representatives of the moral standards of our community, seemed to tolerate without question or debate racially separated religious communities. I viewed these long standing generational practices in my hometown as small snapshots of the larger trend of spiritual and worship exclusivity based on race throughout the nation.

Early in my seminary career, I had the privilege to teach courses on Black Theology and African American religious experience at two predominantly white colleges. One venue was at a Catholic college and the other at a state university. I was taken totally by surprise by the number of non-African American students who enrolled in the course. I was even more surprised by the fact that not one of the non-African American students had ever attended an African American worship service—however, each student expressed to me their wish and willingness to so.

Therefore, as a requirement to pass the courses, I built into the syllabus an African American church visitation exercise. I wanted the students to learn about black worship, but my greater desire was that each student would come to know worship outside of their own tradition, that each would make it a life-long practice to attend a black church as part of their occasional or regular worship experience. This activity also gave me a forum to look closer, to ask questions about religious perceptions; in particular, I could ask questions that offered answers to me regarding the continuing need, or the relevance of racial separation within a religious worship context.

Slavery, its shameful facts, its historical, social and economic inequalities, its damaging impact on the souls and on the psyches of black people, gave birth to the independent black church. Each of these influences was a dominant factor in the rise of sustained institutionalized separate worship communities. These historical conditions shaped the perceptions of both blacks and whites within religious institutions and church life that today represent society in "micro" what is lived in "macro" and are, it appears indicators of intractable vestiges of separation laced within the whole society of American life.

In spite of the clarity and weight of these unalterable facts; at the heart of practiced Christianity by many in America, is the belief that the Bible is truth inerrant. If white Christians and black Christians say they love God, and we all know that His word says we should all love one another, and if that is the truth, then why can't we plow up engrained social behaviors, reach beyond their past constraints and, as "The Church," unconditionally, love one another.

For me, since this does not happen, ultimately more questions are raised: the first, do the consequences of those former historical conditions continue to prohibit blacks and whites from participating fully with one another in a shared worship of God? In order to broach an answer, I had to ask myself the question: what *is* the African American Religious experience? Are there elements in the African American religious experience that are not present in other Christian religious experiences? The next question I probe is that of archetypal alienation. In other words, does an experience with oppression and dehumanization, such as that which impacted blacks for three centuries in America, and was the foundation that formed their worship experience, still impact African Americans in their religious expression in ways that alienate those who have not shared the same or a similar oppressive experience? Then, there is that major religious corollary—the third rail, if you will, of American spirituality—that has to be included in this discussion of major traditions of worship in America: Judaism. Their expression, Judaism's foundational experience, is similar to that of the black tradition of worship.

In this case, I have asked: do those who practice Judaism relate their experience of the persecution of Jews in the Exodus or Holocaust to their religious expressions and experiences in worship? According to Leffler and Jones in their work, *The Structure of Religion: Judaism and Christianity, within Jewish thought,* "Life is sanctified through religious actions, both ritual and ethical. Redemption is connected to the exodus from Egypt."[5]

My work explores these questions through an examination of the immediate religious experiences of both black and white Christians in America, and in a tertiary way, Judaism. Every chapter addresses these questions as they investigate the problems of racial separation of religious worshipers in the following areas: the context of theology and tradition, sacred and secular domains, and in the social context of color and culture.

Too, one must poke about, and I do, to the continuing battle over what consideration is the most important—theology or tradition. It is significant to this discussion that tradition, familial and familiar habits of religious practice are often perceived as having greater validity and authority in the development of the Church's moral and ethical character—that as it relates to racial unity, tradition and family have had more import in forming worship practices than have clear mandates of the Bible and theological principles.

Second, various groups, cultures and religious communities define sacred and secular differently. These differences often overshadow the critical issues related to the meaning and mission of true worship. It is important to observe the particular, "beliefs and practices," and the worship expressions that constitute sacred, as it pertains to religious experience.

The third and final idea looks at perhaps a more serious problem that concerns intra-racial as well as inter-racial relations within religious communities and in society. This is the problem of "color caste." Sadly, this idea encompasses a special kind of spiritual corruption, the politics of color, prevalent over the ages within the black church, and the cultural elements that underlie issues of power, status and individual meaning in black church life. Specifically, this theme makes the argument that historical stereotyping and conditioning has occurred in the minds of both blacks and whites and has proven to be significant factors influencing the separation of worshipers inside the black church.

My contemplation on the issues of spiritual separation and segregation concludes with an exploration and examination of ways in which both the white and black communities can work together to breakthrough the disjointing barriers of religious partitions to build bridges of unity—brotherhood and sisterhood—in the 21st Century Christian Church.

As a former pastor, as an African American man, for nearly two decades, I've had the opportunity to see first hand the unique culture, traditions and styles of worship practiced in the black church. Furthermore, as a director of Black Campus Ministry on two predominately white mid-western universities, as professor at three predominantly white universities, as supply pastor and guest speaker at numerous predominately black and predominately white congregations, I have participated in worship experiences ranging from liturgical to congregational, from highly expressive to formal. I've worked with multicultural student groups for more than a decade, engaging them in Christian worship practices across denominational and non-denominational lines. These have afforded me the unique opportunity to observe spiritual life first hand in the black and white church, and to access and gather data for this work.

The aim of my work is to tender healing, unification; it is not intended to exclude other ethnic or racial groups from this conversation. As well, it seeks to address the ongoing social and historical American dilemma of the black and white racial divide. My hope is that by promoting reconciliation between black and white Christians, others will be inspired to work toward overcoming racial discrimination and barriers on all fronts of social and spiritual interaction; that all across the vast region of American culture and life, committed Christians from all walks of life will rise above the insidious circumstances and the consequences of racial hostilities from the past to face the dawn of a new day where the radiant glow of the Love of Jesus Christ. This is light that will guide us to the blessed land of Christian unity, right here on earth, and Heaven!

NOTES

1. Stream, Carol. Interview with Reverend Dr. Bernice King. "She has a dream, too" Christianity Today (June 16, 1997), 36.

2. James M. Washington, ed. *A Testament of Hope: The Essential Writings and Speeches of Martin Luther King, Jr.* (HarperCollins, New York, 1991), 220.

3. ———. *A Testament of Hope*, 479.

4. New National Baptist Hymnal, "Just as I AM" (National Baptist Publishing Board, 1977), 145.

5. William J. Leffler, II and Paul H. Jones. *The Structure of Religion: Judaism and Christianity* (University Press of America, Inc. Lanham, Maryland:2005), 25.

Chapter One

The Emergence of the Church and its Place in American Society

When the political advances in American institutions are observed, and when achievements in socio-economic arenas and in education are taken into account—the openness, the equality of opportunity, and the representation of all races in the sports and entertainment industry are considered, it is all the more evident that the church is the last vestige of exclusivity where institutional segregation in the society is practiced and accepted.

As soon as the first European settlers arrived to America at Jamestown in the early 1600's and staked the Cross of Christ on the shores of the beach, it became the symbol of the importance religion would play in every sector of American life.

In 1619, the first general assembly of the New World was convened in the Jamestown Church. Its first order of business was to "establish one equal and uniform government over all Virginia." The purpose was to provide "just laws for the happy guiding and governing of the people there inhabiting." At the time of this convention and crafting of its governing decrees, the inhabitants of Jamestown also included the first Africans, who were not then slaves, to have been delivered to the land by a Dutch sailor.[1]

No record is extant of a distinction being made between the "happy governing" of the European inhabitants and the "happy governing" of African inhabitants present in Jamestown. Obviously, people in America, at its earliest stages viewed the concept of inclusiveness as an important aspect of its success. Much later, when the Revolutionary War was fought, it was in part to affirm, to establish and to solidify the freedoms and ideas conceived by those early settlers. As was their desire, one of the primary ideas and ideals was to foster an atmosphere of freedom for the Church, for individuals to have the ability to worship freely, without encumbrances of a religious directive by the state. At that time, there seemed no concept by them to have a Church for the white brethren and one for the Africans who were settling alongside them at Jamestown. America was, therefore, on its way to structuring one of history's greatest experiments in liberty and brotherhood: a unified society where men were assumed to be humane and tolerant of one another and able to self-govern. From all historical evidence; at that moment, the Church was the nucleus of that self-governing society.

At the close of the Revolution, a fledgling democracy, at least in theory, prevailed. The Constitution emerged through long and difficult debates, but yielded: "We hold these truths to be self-evident that all men are created equal and are endowed by their Creator with certain inalienable rights . . ." These, arguably, are the most important words ever to have been written by any person regarding the worth of man and the sanctity of human life. Dr. King, himself, unmatched in the twentieth century as crafter and orator of dynamic words that elevated life and embraced humanity, held these particular words of the nation's forefathers as the bedrock of the Civil Rights Movement and of his humanitarian aspirations. King said, in the "I have a Dream Speech":

> When the architects of our republic wrote the magnificent words of the Constitution and the Declaration of Independence, they were signing a promissory note to which every American was to fall heir. This note was the promise that all men, yes, black men as well as white men, would be guaranteed the unalienable rights of life, liberty, and the pursuit of happiness.[2]

Yet, despite the promise inherent in these ennobling words, it followed that at some point on the grand tapestry of democracy, the concept to "establish one equal and uniform government . . .," was eventually lost in the snares and tragedy of human slavery of the Africans. This act, of taking Africans as chattel, was followed further by the chronological legacy, the entrenchment, and the devastation of authorized segregation of the nation's growing black citizenry. As a result, democracy became a loose garment that was rent and subsequently tortured into a privilege for the few based solely on the color of one's skin. Lost was the belief that democracy was for every individual, a national birthright that is the inherent liberty and freedom intrinsic in life itself, inculcated in the concept of democracy for all human beings. After that fateful ideological change in course, America became one nation with two societies: one black, one white— and the Church, inevitably, was caught in the middle.

The sweeping momentum gathered by the Black Church, along with the demands of the Civil Rights Movement, acknowledged the need not to go idly by, continuing to merely observe and endure the repugnance of the lingering tragedies from the aftermath of slavery. The Movement, in all its profundity, bore witness to, was evidence of how this human disaster continued to unfold;

how it drilled deeper and deeper into the fabric of American life and spirituality. As time passed, the seepage of hatred and racism became more accepted expressions of Church life than the ethics and principles of theology and democracy.

The more that the democratic loss of equality was enshrined in America, these altered concepts of church life and spirituality make fitting for this discussion, a maxim uttered by Reinhold Niebuhr. "There is no social evil, no form of injustice whether of the feudal or the capitalist order, which has not been sanctified in some way or other by religious sentiment and thereby rendered more impervious to change." This saying is applicable to the history of the Christian church throughout the ages. It is especially poignant and can be applied to the state of the Christian church and American social order throughout most of the history of this nation.

As a movement of resistance, in an effort to reopen pathways of entrance and participation in mainstream American life for its constituents, the Black Church had to streamline its spiritual mission to include and address social issues that were hostile to the very existence of its members.

After centuries of being socially excluded and marginalized, the Black Church responded to her indignation; it responded to her plight, Rosa Parks, in Alabama in December 1955. The Black Church rose spiritually to a daunting civic call. The White Church stood by and watched. Part of the responsibility for the existence of racism, separatism in America belongs to The Church. These are the obnoxious offspring of the spiritual bifurcation of protestant Christianity.

The *Letter from a Birmingham Jail* is Dr. Martin Luther King, Jr's. reply to white clergy who complained that he was an "outsider[s] coming in." Said he, Dr. King, was there to "engage in a nonviolent direct-action program if deemed necessary. . ."[3] having been invited by the Reverend Fred Shuttlesworth, and other affiliates of the Alabama Christian Movement for Human Rights. Heeding their call, Dr. King relayed to his white counterparts, that he came in the same spirit of the Prophets who went "beyond the boundaries of their home towns" in response to the prophetic calls of God. Jesus went beyond the boundaries of Galilee to carry the message of liberation and reconciliation of Jews to God. Dr. King pointed out that the disciples, the Apostle Paul and others left their provinces to disseminate the Gospel of Jesus Christ to every far flung corner of the earth.

The White Church was unmoved by the plight of its black brothers and sisters. And so, Dr. King, chided them,

You deplore the demonstrations taking place in Birmingham. But your statement, I am sorry to say, fails to express a similar concern for the conditions that

brought about the demonstrations. I am sure that none of you would want to rest
content with the superficial kind of analysis that deals merely with effects and
does not grapple with underlying causes.[4]

Still, the white clergy and its members were "Like a tree planted by the
rivers of waters,"—they were not moved by Dr. King's impassioned reason
nor did they intend to be. They were not moved by the violence of racism;
they were not moved by the official and civic violence committed against
black people who struggled for the right to obtain justice and to live free in
the society that heralded itself as the world leader of democracy, justice and
freedom.

If white Christians were smug and pleased with their spiritual obstinacy,
black Christians responded with their spiritual obstinacy. They, too, were not
moved. The Black Church was not turned back by the stubbornness of white
Christians and the rest of white society who thought their activities "unwise
and untimely." Their trajectory was to stand like an old oak tree planted by
rivers of deep waters—its roots dug in like those of its white counterparts, because they wanted to be free just like them.

Astonishingly, it was only a decade after Rosa Parks refused to give up her
seat on a city bus in Montgomery, Alabama to a white rider, that comprehen-
sive Civil Rights legislation was signed into law in 1964 by President Lyndon
B. Johnson. These new laws rolled back all of America's desegregation laws,
thanks to the steadfastness of Dr. King's selfless charity and the immoveable
determination of the Black Church to see the mission through; to achieve a
new legacy of civil rights for African Americans.

Since then, America has witnessed enormous progress in race relations. Not
just between blacks and whites, but the entire nation was liberated to be different. It was at liberty to rise above the screeds of segregationist and racist and
the spiritual complacency of white Christians. It was free to rise to the grand
challenges of its creeds of equality, as outlined in the Constitution and the Bill
of Rights, for everyone in the nation. In fact, it is apparent that the nation had
become liberated enough to fall back on the roots of its spiritual genesis.

To speak of spiritual genesis, a spiritual revival of sorts, followed close on
the heels of the Civil Rights Movement. In 1967, a spiritual awakening in the
Haight Asbury section of San Francisco called the Jesus Movement swept the
country and brought together, by its doctrines of spiritual renewal, black and
white Christians in common worship.[5]

Again, in the 1970's, the Charismatic Movement found a secure starting
point in the nation's Christian circles. Its chief aim was to bridge the gap between various protestant groups and Catholics. However, without comment-
ing on the theological merits of these movements, their "newness" created a

conduit of inclusiveness for Christians across the ethnic spectrum that was heretofore rare in protestant circles.

The spiritual and worship constructs that were formed by the "revivals" were called "non-denominational." At the outset, these new worship communities lacked the rigidity, the structure and the organizational affiliations of mainstream Christianity. Nonetheless, they managed to flourish. They pulled into its ranks new members from across the racial spectrum, and offered an alternative to blacks and whites who had previously belonged to mainstream black and white churches.

I do not hesitate to connect this new phenomenon of Christian liberty and vitality of worship directly to the enormous progress that was made in race relations just after the close of the Civil Rights Movement. Many white preachers who were no where to be found in the struggle to gain civil rights for their black brother and sisters now felt "called of God" to create new churches within this atmosphere of this refreshed spiritual liberty. They benefited tremendously from the struggles of Dr. King's vision and thrust for racial and spiritual accountability and change. In great numbers, black worshippers flocked to these gatherings for an "infilling of the Spirit," and to hear a brand new "revelation of the word."

This post Civil Rights vision for the church, this positive vibrancy of the so-called "prophetic" ministry was most definitely a catalyst to inter-racial worship and has, since the late 1960's, helped to redefine the Church as we move into the 21st century. Blacks, whites and other ethnic groups are not only free today to worship together, but they are comfortable doing so. In what was once an unconventional setting socially, spiritually and racially, this gifting of black members into these new white congregations early on did not go unnoticed by black leaders. There was concern voiced about the spiritual well-being of black congregants with white pastors and naturally so. Along with that concern, there was an undertow of resentment—hence more separation—by black pastors about the exodus of black Christians into the ranks of white churches.

I was impressed during a recent visit to Southern California, while thumbing through the Yellow Pages looking for a place to worship, by the number of congregations that were listed as multicultural worship communities. The advent and growth of these centers are the progeny of Dr. King's spiritual foresight. They demonstrate the naturalness of inclusion. It is my belief that many churchgoers tend toward racial inclusion rather than the opposite. What might have hindered people from seeking integrated worship before was that they lacked the forum to step outside the boundaries of the politics of exclusivity or a family tradition of worship to make inclusiveness happen. A more open and accepting society on issues of race provided that forum for them, and aided by men and women church leaders who seized upon the prospect at the conclusion of Dr. King's work, that helped Christians to make inclusiveness in worship another aspect of a new social and worship tapestry.

When new civil rights laws abolished old racially restrictive ones, that was the key that unlocked the door to new access in American society for blacks; however, some institutions, and many common citizens were not ready to throw away the padlock that kept the country operating like an elite country club.

As well, just after the Civil Rights Movement, the American demography began to shift, to be reshaped. With equal housing opportunities now available to blacks, many began to wish for life in better houses and wanted to move into neighborhoods better than their old neighborhoods.

Not surprisingly, the banks responded with redlining practices, exorbitant rates, or by making it as hard for blacks as possible to get loans to improve their housing. Dual lending practices—though they were now illegal according to federal law, for a while, succeeded to keep blacks out of houses in modest neighborhoods that were previously all white. Blacks, who were not welcomed at the bank, but who did manage to get a loan and to get a house in a better neighborhood, were not welcomed in the new neighborhoods. Some new black homeowners were terrorized by hate crimes, by rude or bullying neighbors, but the typical response around the country to black neighbors by white homeowners was to pack up and move into other neighborhoods, those more expensive, where there were no blacks.

This is the fact: many whites were committed not to share the landscape, the good of the land, in any way, with blacks. Whites began to leave the urban areas in droves and to take comfort in a world of refuge—in "white flight." New sprawling suburbs were built to accommodate this new ideology of separation. White congregations, which had anchored communities for generations moved to areas outlying cities. Edifices of former white churches became large gaping hulks, abandoned, in cities where blacks were becoming more mobile. Some of those churches were purchased by black congregations, but many soon fell into disrepair because of the economic burden of keeping them maintained. Many urban areas became all black, and blighted as whites sought new and cleverer ways to resist, resent the changes, to ignore the existence of a black population in America. Deserted white churches trumpeted a loud and sad commentary on the spiritual state of American Christianity.

On the other hand, many mainstream white Christians did not flee locales from cities and towns that were making possible a new way of life for blacks. Model City projects were under way, jobs training programs were underway, open entry college admissions, and student loans were making it possible for many blacks to pursue a higher education, and minority set asides were making it possible for blacks to compete for lucrative government contracts. While white congregations that remained in the cities did not go out of their way to actively recruit black members, some did become more responsive to the spiritual realities of black life and the needs of this people. It is not apparent that they did anything to disparage or hinder the new civic and economic opportunities being offered to change the lives of African Americans.

I am not suggesting at all in this work the abolishment of the Black Church or the White Church. What I am suggesting is that if black Christians and white Christians lay aside their differences, and instead, lay down their lives for one another, and pick up an act of biblical significance, "Greater love hath no man than this . . . that a man should lay down his life for his friends."[6] Jesus told his disciples that they would be identified by this selfless act—by their demonstration of love for one another.

What I am suggesting, therefore, is that black Christians and white Christians should be willing and able to come together routinely for fellowship, for spiritual vetting, for mapping social harmony, to discuss how they can participate in united worship of a true and loving God. These actions would follow in the noble footsteps of Martin Luther King, Jr. who walked in the footsteps of Jesus. He laid down his life for his brothers, in an act of redemption, sacrifice and reconciliation. Joint fellowship would be a practice that honors the lives of black and white Christians, one that honors true worship; and that, honors Christ.

As we enter the 21st century, an unsettling erosion of the gains of the Civil Rights Movement is and has been apparent for a couple of decades. In the 1980's, the country took a dramatic shift to a more conservative posture. People became comfortable during the Regan era to move away from the "liberalism" of a Great Society. Many black leaders squandered the gains realized through hard fought Civil Rights Movement of the 50's and 60's, not fully understanding the magnanimity of the Movement, and its significance to future inheritors. America rested on its spiritual and civic laurels as if the work of spiritual and civic restoration had been completed, and mainstream Christianity was still absent and silent on these concerns.

After the death of Dr. King, no solid voice of leadership emerged, even from his own circles, to move the country forward. There still has been no defined moral, humanitarian, or civic compass that nurtures and enlarges upon his gains. What did arise, however, were a cacophony of voices that exploited the rewards of the Civil Rights Movement, rather than build on them, or to contribute to them; but none has arisen, even to this day, that is capable of moving the big Dream forward despite the apparent and desperate need of the country to move toward full equalitarian values. As a result; America, in spirit and attitude, has drifted back into the complacency of a separate but unequal society.

Separation and inequality are no longer legally sanctioned or mandated by a majority of the culture—but the presence and effects of invisible segregation are every bit as destructive as the social and spiritual virulence which scourged the country for the majority of its 230 years.

A recent Harvard report points to the fact that school desegregation nationwide, specifically in grades K-12, is on the rise. The aftermath of Hurricane Katrina revealed in horrific starkness how huge is the gap between the rich and the poor—between those who have and between those who do not have, almost exclusively along racial lines, consequently, blacks are the majority of those that "do not have."

Whether black worshippers are in Harlem, New York, or whether white worshipers are in Billings, Montana—of course, there is a difference in location, spiritual needs, and what is needed and expected from their individual worship communities—the challenges of getting each need met for each individual parishioner is the primary yet enormous challenge of a dynamic transformative Christian community. Nonetheless, there is a clamorous wake up call that is sounding, and The Church is snoozing right through it.

The proliferation of hate crimes against blacks in the latest reported statistics show there were more of such crimes committed against blacks than against any other American minority group. According to *People's Daily Online*, The FBI Hate Crime Statistics issued in October 2005 stated, "of the 9,528 victims of hate crimes in 2004, 53.8 percent were victims of racial prejudice, and 67.9 percent were blacks. Among the hate crime offenders, 60.6 percent were whites."[7] In his February 2005 article, "*FBI Reports Increase in Hate Crimes Against African Americans*" Russell Malik, for The Crisis wrote that, "hate crimes against African Americans were nearly twice that of all other race groups combined." This ominous reality included four murders. The source of Malik's information was the FBI report, "Hate Crimes Statistics. 2003." Moreover, statistics also show that blacks are twenty times more likely than whites to be victims of hate crimes.

Nearly 100,000 blacks die annually because they lack health insurance; blacks are unemployed at the rate of 10.6 percent as compared to their white counterparts at 4.3 percent.[8] Racial profiling and police brutality continues unabated as the country moves along the first decade of the 21st century. In a report issued by the Center for Policy Alternatives, in 2005 "a report by the U.S. Department of Justice found that police were significantly more likely to carry out some type of search on an African American (10.2 percent) than on a white driver (3.5 percent). This same report states that, "African Americans and Latinos were three times more likely to experience force or threat of force during a police stop."[9]

Obviously, with these kinds of murky findings, the commitment to fill the breach in America's racial divide is lacking leadership in every sector of the population. It goes without saying that not enough is being done to do so. These are sober reminders that there are legitimate reasons for the fears and suspicions among African Americans about whether America can make good on the promises of a free, equal and just society.

The racial past of America is painful, it impregnates the present with doubts and it unfairly barters the future of every American with distorted images of one another, and with fear and mistrust. What is more, it taints the views of African Americans who reject outright the notion that large numbers of white Christians are committed to social equality, or that they are willing to boldly embrace the biblical concepts of unity, unfeigned love of all people, reconciliation and brotherhood, when it comes to religion and principles of justice, they are often silent.

If silence appears to parody consent for white Christians on racial equality; certainly, this is not the time for African Americans to become weary, for that would parody defeat, and consent of another type. This is not the time for the Church—black or white to retreat into social conformity. Both organizations, if moved out of the cocoon of tradition, suspicion, nostalgia, and their unremitting addiction to spiritual comfort, an unrelenting resistance to change, they might, together, assume their rightful place in the forefront as vanguards of human rights, as protectors of freedom and liberty in America. Each community is needed, right now, to step up to the task.

NOTES

1. Kirk D. Kehrberg Park Ranger, Colonial NHP, "The First Legislative Assembly at Jamestown, Virginia," Colonial National Historical Park 1999, http://www.nps.gov/colo/jthanout/1stASSLY.html (July 25,2006).

2. ———. *A Testament of Hope*, 217.

3. ———. *A Testament of Hope,* 289.

4. ———. *A Testament of Hope,* 290.

5. The Hollywood Free Paper, "A brief history of the Jesus Movement,"2006, http://www.hollywoodfreepaper.org/portal.php?id=2 July, 26, 2006).

6. *John 15:13, KJV.*

7. Malik Russell, "FBI Reports Increase in Hate Crimes Against African Americans," The Crisis, Jan/Feb 2005, http://www.findarticles.com/p/articles/mi_qa4081/is_ai_n9522077 (Jan/Feb 2005).

8. People's Daily Online, "Racial discrimination in U.S. serious, says report," http://english.people.com.cn/200603/09/eng20060309_249225.html (9 March, 2006).

9. Center for Policy Alternatives: Racial Profiling.xm http://www.cfpa.org/issues/issue/RacialProfiling.xml (6 July, 2006).

Chapter Two

The Role of the Black Church in a Fragmented Society

The Civil Rights Movement is a fine example of the fact that the state needs no protection from the church, but that the church can provide protections for the state and its citizenry. The strategies of the modern Civil Rights Movement were successful in gaining a measure of parity for African Americans barred by centuries of discrimination from participating in the social and political processes of America.

As imagined by George Washington, father of the Revolution, and first to lead the nation, America was to be as a place where Asians, Africans and Europeans could come to America and freely pursue the chosen course of their lives. This was clearly his thinking as he along with the other founders pondered what this country would represent — what its identity would mean to the world and to people of all religions, people of no religion, of any people, regardless of national origin who inhabited it. Steven Kautz reflected Washington's sentiments when he said,

> Tolerance is a liberal virtue: it is among the most honorable of respectable habits of liberal habits of liberal citizens. Here is the noble promise of "enlarged and liberal policy" of toleration, in President Washington's famous words: that among us "every one shall sit in safety under his own vine and fig-tree, and there shall be none to make him afraid"; that here the community will give "to bigotry no sanction, to persecution no assistance" (Letter to the Hebrew Congregation of Newport, 1790).[1]

Washington understood the gravity of his visionary astuteness; that it would be a grand undertaking to craft a nation of one from a disparate pallet of many. Like Solomon, many centuries before him — he knew that it would be a task unlike any other to guide the nation in principals of government with its main stipulation to be respect for the rights of every individual. George Washington saw no reason or circumstances under which all people should not be able to live and work as freemen in America. At a time during the Revolution, to his soldiers—who were black men and white men—he said,

> The time is now near at hand which must probably determine, whether Americans are to be, freemen or slaves; whether they are to have any property they can call their own . . . The fate of unborn millions will now depend, under God, on the courage and conduct of this army . . . Let us therefore rely on the goodness of the cause and the aid of the Supreme Being, in whose hands victory is, to animate and encourage us to greater and noble actions.[2]

After many recorded strange and miraculous interventions during the War, the Revolution was won. Washington's success helped to establish this great nation on a course unlike that of any other on the earth. When he took his oath of office for the presidency on April 30, 1789, he did not cease to demonstrate his pious reliance on God. He was the first president to say the perennial four word prayer, "So help me God," beseeched by every other, at his inauguration, since then.

Usually, when secular writers chronicle George Washington's legacy, they omit any mention of his Christian devotion. When religious writers write about our first president, they fail to mention that Washington's personal success was connected to his prolific involvement in slavery. With this paradox in mind, Washington's thoughts on freedom and liberty have to be extolled with a perilous caveat. And if honesty is to be at the center of reporting history and its influence on the present, neither fact can be ignored. The glorious truth herein is that our first president and founder was a pious man who loved God and his country. The disturbing truth is that this same man owned 316 slaves.

According to the Mount Vernon's Ladies Association, all of Washington's slaves were freed by him in his last will and testament. Many were provided for by him, and some were educated by his final wishes. It is speculated that slaveholding was an issue which came to trouble Washington greatly—it was in direct opposition to his goals for the nation. And it is no wonder, for it was he who wrote, "Let us with caution indulge the supposition that morality can be maintained without religion. Reason and experience both forbid us to expect that national morality can prevail in exclusion of religious principle"[3] — still, slavery was an issue on which he took no public stand. Certainly, it is too his credit that Washington freed his slaves before he died. All the same, when one considers the permanent impact and influence of his life on the nation for the good that he did, who is to say where the nation might be today had he refused to own slaves during his lifetime.

George Washington was born into a society where slavery was practiced and accepted. I venture to suggest, though, that the nation might have taken a much different direction had he risked the political fallout, and denounced the practice while he governed. He saw America as the land of promise, but caution on the issue may have helped to validate the institution of slavery and invalidate the intrinsic worth of the lives of its dark skinned citizens.

Weaved out of slavery, the sagging garment of racial apartheid called Jim Crow was an ugly bird, heavy with racism and discrimination in its wings, it flew, like a scepter, over the lives of millions of blacks until the advent of social movements that resisted it. The modern Civil Rights Movement was not the first to address on a large scale the inequities of racism, it was, however, the most visible and the most successful aimed at ending the decimations of injustice. In shaping the objectives of the Movement, it was the black clergy who became the representatives of the protests. They were the ones in the forefront of the movement to articulate the objections black people felt and had held back for generations.

His voice is permanently engraved in our hearts and upon history; and one can see and cannot help but appreciate the impact of Dr. Martin Luther King's spirited oratory—it was an agent of change. The voices of other black preachers: my friend, Fred Shuttlesworth, Andrew Young, Joseph Lowery, Jesse Jackson, and other clergymen willing to make the personal sacrifices needed to push for the rights of a nation of distressed black people, became the public faces, the often heard public voices of the Civil Rights Movement.

The language of the Civil Rights Movement was the language of religion, of civic rebellion and patriotism. This seems like an unlikely mix of ideologies, though these were they that spearheaded the language of the Black Church to show its resilience. The Black Church became more progressive, it showed its previously dormant strength, and empowered itself economically. It took care of its members and moved with more determination than ever before, to jolt America into becoming the democracy its Declarations said it must be.

The Black Church had to reaffirm itself to numerous members of its role as an ark of refuge for them, a place where they could find shelter from a hostile white world. The Black Church could be this rock of refuge because it was free to operate as an entity free of outside interference, completely owned by blacks and wholly identified with their lives, their culture, their sorrows, their spiritual needs, and now their hopes and aspirations for social parity and political access. This was the black experience, the Christ likeness of the black church; of its spirit and its identity. This was the role of the Black Church in a fragmented society throughout its history and up to 1964 when African Americans were, in a sense, grafted anew into the provisions already given them by the Constitution of the United States of America. The tradition of the black church was to nurture the spirits of black worshippers and to protect them; its role was to survive the social conditions by which it was oppressed.

The black leaders of the Black Church had to shift their roles somewhat, in that era to reaffirm themselves, externally, as spokespersons for social unity and internally as spiritual leaders who encouraged their members to look to God—to stand fast—not to be moved by what they saw, nor by what they heard, or by what they experienced in the struggle for their God given rights to be free in America.

NOTES

1. Steven Kautz, "Liberalism and the Idea of Toleration," American Journal of Political Science, Vol.37, No.2 (May, 1993):610-632.

2. Phyllis Schlafly, "George Washington's Advise," Eagle Forum *http://www.usiap. org/Legacy/Quotes?George Washington.html* (13 July 2006).

3. James F. Gauss, *We the People, Volume II: Birth of a Nation (Bloomington, IN: Lightning Source, Inc.)* 2004.

Chapter Three

The American Family, Church Tradition and Theology

In America, if you are white and are a member of a mainstream religious worship tradition; going to church, worship means one thing. In America, if you are black and are a member of a black religious tradition; going to church, worship means another thing all together.

An avid abolitionist, John Wesley stirred the religious passions of slaves with his "plain doctrine and good discipline" into the ranks of Methodism among whites. White Methodists of the time, however, were uncomfortable with the presence of blacks in their services. At Philadelphia's St. George's Methodist Church, in November 1787 white church leaders unceremoniously and vehemently discriminated against Richard Allen, Absalom Jones and their constituents compelling them to leave St. George's church.[1] Surely, this action, while worship was in progress laid the ground work for the long standing schism rent between black and white Christians. It may be the link that established a pattern of unkind discord that has never been tended to and that has never been fixed. During the 1950's and the 1960's amid the spiritual push of the Civil Rights Movement for spiritual transparency and accountability, the differences between the two worship communities and their intentions crystallized even more.

For centuries, and certainly not since the eighteenth century, have these two religious traditions tried to come together universally to, again, mean anything common, spiritually connected, or moderate. Neither group has sought motives within biblical constraints to build bridges that move their respective worshipers toward the common goal of pulling the band-aid off the deep and penetrating wounds of fear, bigotry and racism; indifference and the inability to thoroughly forgive. The power of authentic cleansing and transforming faith has not been explored; rather, these principals of godliness continue, indeed, to be ignored by both groups. The perennial separation of black Christians and white Christians means that the boundaries of the separate traditions continue to solidify. Today, there is no apparent or outright hostility between the black church and the white church; however, that there are still the two ongoing and separate societies, support the ugly reality of no specific agenda for reconciliation from both sectors.

It is often that I hear from Christians, whites and blacks alike, "What difference does it make if white folk don't want to worship with black folk, or if black folk don't want to worship with white folk?" My answer to this so flippantly asked question is: "Nothing would be wrong with any of this if all were well in the doing." Clearly, Matthew 11:25, "And when ye stand praying, forgive, if you have ought against any: that your Father also which is in heaven may forgive your trespasses.,"[2] is a primary requisite for right standing with God, and for right standing with one another. Yet, it is outside this mandated clarity of spiritual consciousness that motivates blacks and whites to separate for worship.

Instead, combined with all the other historical factors, the separation is rooted partially in the superficial cloak of ethnic identity, historical tradition, and styles of worship. Hence, for blacks, their argument is, "Black folk need to hold on to their way of worship." 'Although the black community is not monolithic, all do not worship the same; their mode of worship is often stereotyped as the most elemental and unsophisticated. There is the universal tendency to assign the taste and conduct of some to the taste and conduct of all. This is elemental—this is racism—even many blacks ascribe to this notion in error.'[3]

The popularity of the Charismatic Movement proves that religious expressiveness and emotional involvement in worship is not limited to the black church and that such behavior is not an exclusively ethnic event; still, I've heard some whites say, "That Gospel music is just too loud and emotionally charged," hence, an excuse by whites to continue to marginalize blacks and to access platitudes necessary to continue to forge two societies. That black worshippers might not be able to be "expressive" in what they consider to be the "stoic" white church; that the white worshipper may be somewhat put off by the more "emotional" black service are flimsy arguments. They are pseudo-theologies that are supported by family traditions, cultural traditions and a brand of religion that promote the will of self. They are, though, genuinely effective smokescreens.

This kind of thinking keeps blacks from being moved—it keeps whites moored in their places. And, so, worshippers from both traditions, glibly ignore eternal truths, and adhere to the dark and forceful doctrines of the past. A seemingly irreparable fissure runs straight through the middle of the

Church and each says they see no real contradiction in the practice of separate worship. They say that regardless of race, worshipers may separate—that race should not be a factor in whether or not to do so, "It's really about nothing more than tradition."

According to Leonard Steinhorn and Barbara Diggs-Brown, "nearly nine in ten black church members nationwide belong to black denominations such as the African Methodist Episcopal Church or the National Baptist Convention."[4] In as much as tradition can and perhaps has gotten in the way of progress and healing between blacks and whites, they have chosen to overlook the gnarly past that bred this tradition. It appears that after four hundred year old roots have grown so deeply into the soil of their hearts, most whites and most blacks never see the faces of one another in the church pews on Sunday mornings, and neither is greatly troubled about it.

Ironically, a failure to achieve unity, community and love are contradictory to the scripture. God we cannot see; and yet, we say we love Him. On the other hand, black Christians and white Christians, on a significant scale, don't harvest the inspiration from week to week to love one another with that same love for God; that is, not enough to pursue genuine brotherhood with one another, or to tackle their obvious problems of mutual and benign spiritual neglect. This rift is a tradition, but it is a tradition of man and not of God. The Apostle Paul uses physical anatomy to describe just how cohesive the Church should be: The eye cannot say to the hand, I do not need you; nor the head to the feet, I do not need you" (I Corinthians 12:21). Does anyone suppose that black and white Christians feel more comfortable obeying man and tradition and not God and His will? What Do Christians Value More: Tradition or Theology?

To try and answer this question, one need only look at the facts to understand that family, culture and tradition intertwine in such a way that people begin to believe that their tradition is the will of God. They settle into the theology or theologies provided by their tradition, which makes it necessary for me to clarify what I mean by theology contextually in this work.

Theology, and sometimes more than one theology describes a system of religious beliefs held in common by a group of people by which they are instructed, or by which they govern their organization; by which they talk about God or some other worshiped deity. I use the theology of Judeo-Christian doctrines [based on the teachings of the Old Testament and on the teachings of Jesus Christ] to examine race relations and the Church in America. My aim is to gauge how Christianity was conceptualized and practiced through the ages and how now, it is conceptualized and conducted in our post-modern society where Christianity is bed rocked in tradition; but, has also grown to have numerous additional denominational and non-denominational affiliations.

In his book, Robert R. Schreiter, *Constructing Local Theologies* observed that there has been a shift in perspectives in theology in recent years. "While the basic purpose of theological reflection has remained the same—namely, the reflection of Christians upon the gospel in light of their own circumstances—much more attention is now being paid to how those circumstances shape the response to the gospel."[5] In James Cone's work, *For My People: Black Theology and the Black Church,* he provides a concise Christian theological framework in which to discuss racial issues and the Christian Church. He stated: "If God is the creator of all persons and through Christ has made salvation possible for everyone, why are some oppressed and segregated in the churches and in society on the basis of color?"[6] The work of Schreiter suggests such a personalization of the gospel hat is conducive to the creation of a narrow myopic perspective. This approach can advocate spiritual isolation, if the scope of the gospel is limited to personal interests alone. The work of Cone, like many African Americans, detects straightforward racism in the way Christianity is practiced today. These two lucid observers convey ideas that suggest the ways and traditions of Christians are anomalous to the love and unity envisioned by Christ; they are an anomaly to the structure of the Church as envisioned by the Apostle Paul.

If tradition is the handing down of customs from one generation to another, then the handed down tradition of separation of religious worshippers on the basis of race and ethnicity is one that is in direct contradiction to the prayer of Jesus in John's gospel—"that they may be one" (John 17:20-21). American Christianity has failed to live up to this grand ideal intended to liberate believers and any society that considers itself great. A great society would embrace its pluralism with a synthesis of tolerance—just as Jesus demonstrated when he walked through Samaria. Instead, the "theology of tradition" has produced a Christian society of exclusivity and intolerance. Of course, the separation of Christian worshippers according to race and ethnicity is not grounded in the truth of the Bible. It is rather grounded in historical animus that defies the very nature of the Church and its meaning.

According to Peter J. Paris, ". . . the white churches reflected in their thought and practice the same interracial relations that characterized society as a whole,"[7] and concomitantly, with this stance justified religiously and morally the immoral separation of the races in the Church of Jesus Christ. Though the course of Paris' argument revolves around the 18th and 19th century black church, his perspective is valid in this discussion because it brings to bear, and necessarily contrast in the contemporary recalcitrance of the black church to include in its thrust for Civil Rights; understandably, this would not be easy, greater momentum and challenge to the white Church for reconciliation and integration of the two religious communities.

Correctly, George Barna states in the introduction of his book, The *Second Coming of the Church,* "Churches have neither adapted their ministries to serve the needs of different ethnic groups nor demonstrated leadership in eliminating racial tensions heightened by America's escalating ethnic diversity."[8] At the end of the 20th century, President William Jefferson Clinton was compelled to call upon the Church to lead the way in the country to build bridges to span the racial divide. If not the Church, then to whom should the president have turned? Certainly, the Church should be the leader, the honest broker in leading the way to reconciliation on all levels, and not just on race either, in precept and example.

That is why Paul said in his letter to the Galatians, "There is neither Jew nor Greek, there is neither bond nor free, there is neither male nor female: for you are all one in Christ Jesus (3:28). In spite of Paul's admonition, the "theology of tradition" brings with it those outdated and erroneous historical perceptions that both blacks and whites have concerning one another. As tragic as is the separation of the Church in the 21st century, no part of this history of tradition presents as too ugly to continue; nor is it powerful enough to convict the hearts of those who might spur change—to end the tradition and /or the theology of separation—which, in light of the fact that neither blacks nor whites seem willing to do; the racial separation of worshipers, has actually attained its own shameful status of theology.

Sammy Tippit acknowledges in his work, *The Choice: America at the Crossroads of Ruin and Revival,* "The culture in which we grew up taught us that blacks weren't our equals. We went through forced integration during high school. Many of us were taught to oppose any attempt of African Americans to enter our schools, and we were taught not to have friendships with black young people."[9]

Needless to say, what Tippit admits to in his upbringing was not a unique experience of familial indoctrination. This kind of intransigent and virulent prejudice and racial stereotyping was conventional and is an intentional and deliberate method of passing on the tradition of racism. Its intended result was social bifurcation, and the strategy was not new to Tippit's generation and did not end in it. Rampant throughout America, this vapid mindset has impacted theological reflections and interracial perceptions for a very long time. However, Tippit's honesty signals a need for new, and long overdue, theological thinking and it is a clarion call for revival. How do black and white Christians pick this kind of status quoism out of the language of their theology?

Well, Tony Evans states that, "There is no more time for us to sit passively and wait for people to change. People must be led into change, and that cannot be done without the knowledge that we will be held accountable for how we treat the other members of God's family."[10] Leonard Steinhorn adds more, "In communities across America, there are infrequent but heart-warming examples of all-white and all-black churches holding interracial services around Easter or the Martin Luther King Holiday. This is the way it should look every Sunday. . ."[11]

Gardener C. Taylor, a Baptist minister born in Louisiana in 1918, wrote prophetically concerning racial prejudice in America, when he said, "The Church of Jesus Christ might well now bow its head in America, for it, North and South, led in promoting the ceremonies and rituals which institutionalized and shaped the contours of this evil."[12] While other institutions have been moved, often gradually and often by force of federal and state courts, to achieve institutional integration, the Church of Jesus Christ still remains the last holdout in society on the frontier of intentional inclusion and unity.

The tradition of separate churches for separate races identifies the poor spiritual and moral health of the Church. When the church fails to address this serious issue of racial segregation among the churches from all points, then it actively engages in the formation of a doctrine of separation. Unless the Church addresses the history of the tradition to its perpetuation, starting with the ground floor of the Sunday morning worship service—how that looks or doesn't look when believers gather to worship, but most important, as honest brokers of a biblical prospective that submits to what the Bible has to say about Christian unity; under these circumstances, the Church gives tacit ascent to and formulates the acceptance of the actions and values of the people within its particular community on the subject. I believe that it is accurate for me to assert that to which churches acquiesces in silence is that which they condone. Subjects against which the churches fail to oppose or speak against are those to which they actively concede.

NOTES

1. Albert J. Raboteau. *Canaan Land: A Religious History of African Americans* (Oxford University Press, New York, 2001), 23.

2. *Matthew 11:25. KJV*

3. Samuel DeWitt Proctor, *The Substance of Things Hoped For: A Memoir of African-American Faith* (Judson Press, Valley Forge, PA: 1995), 192.

4. Leonard Steinhorn and Barbara Diggs-Brown. *By The Color of our Skin: The Illusion of Integration and the Reality of Race* (A Plume Book, New York, 1999), 63.

5. Robert R. Schreiter, *Constructing Local Theologies* (Mary Knoll, NY: Orbis, 1986), 1.

6. James Cone, *For My People: Black Theology and the Black Church* (Mary Knoll, N.Y. Orbis, 1984), 5.

7. Peter J. Paris, *The Social Teaching of the Black Churches* (Fortress Press, Philadelphia, 1985), 45.

8. George Barna, *The Second Coming of the Church* (Word Publishing, Nashville, 1998), 3.

9. Sammy Tippit, *The Choice: America at the Crossroads of Ruin and Revival* (Moody Press, Chicago 1998), 28-29.

10. Tony Evans, *Are Blacks Spiritually Inferior to Whites: Dispelling of an American Myth* (Renaissance Productions, Inc. Wenonah, NJ: 1992), 141.

11. Leonard Steinhorn and Barbara Diggs-Brown, *By The Color of our Skin* (A Plume Book, New York, 1999) 63.

12. Alfred T. Davies, Ed. *The Pulpit Speaks on Race* (Abingdon Press, NY: 1965).

Chapter Four

Sacred, Secular, or Merely Sinful

All Christians know God as the giver of life—"That in Him was life; that life was the light of men." (John 1:3). Most Christians fully understand that only God can give life; that everyone alive has been given this one time unrepeatable experience on earth by Him. It stands to reason that since God created all life, then all life is precious to Him. His act of creating and giving life is Holy; therefore all life is sacred.

Of this knowledge, many Christians act fully unaware where it concerns religion, or when it involves shared worship practices. Sometimes, it is as if they deliberately seal their hearts off from the truth that God is no respecter of persons, or it is that they simply refuse to acknowledge this truth when it involves "their church."

From my fellowship with, and observation of contemporary followers of Christ, there seems to be an ability in their belief and behavior to parse the word sacred in such a way that it has more to do the institutional practices of the Church, with that which is external, more so than it has to do with matters of the heart and spirit; of any intimacy and connection at all to the life, truth and holiness of God and His word.

Rudolf Otto uses "holy and sacred interchangeably and defines these terms like this: "holy" should be understood as ". . . 'the [presentation of] the gradual shaping and filling in with ethical meaning, or what we call the 'schematization,' of what was a unique original feeling-response, which can be in itself ethically neutral and claims consideration in its own right."[1] In other words, sacred might be a uniquely inward experience, a response to the inner realizations of a precious inner life in response to moments with God, moments that gain clarity and deeper formation as one walks with Him. Conversely, Emile Durkheim, in *The Elementary Forms of Religious Life*, considers, "sacred in terms of things being set apart, forbidden, beliefs and practices which unite into one single moral community called a church."[2] So therefore, in light of his view, it is important to observe the particular "beliefs and practices" that constitute the religious experiences Christians interpret as sacred. To them, the term "Church" generally evokes the activities of singing, preaching, and fellowship among those of like beliefs, isolated to their familiar circle. And, likewise, it is obvious that most people, who are usually closely bonded with their "church", are able to conceive of their institution as a sacred place. They are able to conceive mentally or emotionally of the reality of God, whom they believe is holy and deem to be head of their institution in organizational declarations. Yet, in all this, there is only an oblique connection with the Spirit of God as it relates to a truly sacred interchange with His life as conducted through His word. In this manner, the beliefs and practices of the Church supersedes the sacredness of God's word and the life it gives. The result is that God is strangely distant in the midst of a gathering of Christians who are able to hold tenaciously to their traditions, to the exclusion of everything and everyone different than them; this is profane, and without a prick to their conscious.

An aspect of what both black and white Christians hold to be sacred and which they may not want to share or relinquish is their traditional style of worship. Michael O. Emerson and Christian Smith found in their study, *Divided by Faith*, that some whites prefer a separation of worship because of the way worship is conducted. One of their white respondents admitted that, ". . . the way we express our worship to God is different. And so if I choose to worship the way I enjoy worshiping, and my black brothers and sisters want to worship in another fashion that should be okay."[3] As much as worshipers want to believe that their style of worship is sacred, it is probably safe for me to say that neither black styles, nor white styles may be considered sacred. In as much as both practices are largely outgrowths of secular experiences, worship practices are temporal and are the interpreted expressions of our daily contact with the temporal world.

During worship, Black worshipers are free to expel their disillusionment with life through their emotions when in church; whites on the other hand possess the same cool reserve and stoic confidence that is reminiscent of their understanding that the society in which black worshipers are so frustrated; there, they dominate, there they have free course.

The fact remains though that historically, during the development of the Free Church Movement, white Methodist and white Baptists who came to the early camp meetings experienced emotional, expressive forms of worship and responded to the activities of the services by showing some levels of emotional unity that crossed racial lines. The fact that these white worshipers were socially and economically marginalized similarly as oppressed blacks meant that they had the 'psychic and emotional needs that qualitatively did not vastly differ from those of black slaves.'[4] Winthrop S. Hudson details the religious behavior of the white Protestant revivalist this way,

> With 'the traditionally slow cycle of guilt, despair, hope and assurance being compressed into a few days or even hours, the emotional stress was agonizingly intensified and it cut deep into normal restraint. Not only were there outbursts of weeping and shouts of joy; in the frenzied excitement of the moment individuals were suddenly swept into physical "exercises"—falling, running, jumping, jerking—which were attributed to the smiting power of the Holy Spirit.[5]

It is not difficult to imagine that upon the presence of the Holy Spirit entering such meetings, He might have gone unnoticed in the tumult; likewise, in a chilly emotionless atmosphere void of any expression, His appearance might also go unrecognized.

Robert Webber says that, "In Church, his body, there are tangible signs of the presence of Christ in Worship—the assembled people, the Word, the sacraments, ministry, fellowship, discipleship, prayer and love. All these expressions of worship look back to the Christ event and forward to the new heaven and the new earth."[6] Of love, especially, should worship be a Christ-like expression; for, in the context of Christ's teachings, love is an act of self-abandonment. It is sacred in its dynamism and in its execution. Love excludes no one. And, surely, each group must know that God has the power to heal that which is wounded; to bind that which is broken. Unless He is earnestly sought to heal the racial rift in the Church, there remains a spiritual rift with Him from both sides.

In Hoyt Hickman's work on worship, *A Primer for Church Worship*, he says, "In the nineteenth and twentieth centuries, Protestant worship in American has gone through several phases."[7] The first phase was characterized by an emphasis on preaching, evangelism and church growth. This period also included congregational singing, hymns and songs filled with biblical imagery. The second phase Hickman identified as "The high church" or aesthetic or romantic movement that developed in England in the nineteenth century and became increasingly popular in American Protestant churches in the early and middle twentieth century."[8]

This second phase was characterized by elaborate and ritualistic forms of worship. The liturgies included printed prayers. "There was a concern to enrich worship, to restore old traditions, to offer to God the most beautiful music and liturgies and art."[9] Hickman believes that the third phase which occurred in the sixties and seventies, and I suppose well into the eighties, was the contemporary or experimental phase of worship. "Readings might be from contemporary sources as well as from scripture, songs might be anything current (religious or secular) which reflected the people's feelings or the world they lived in. . ."[10]

Another observer of church worship is James F. White, who states in his book, *Protestant Worship: Traditions in Transition,* that "Worship traditions are never static, especially when dominated by the Holy Spirit!"[11] The history of American Protestant worship upholds White's notion that styles and expressions of what might be viewed as sacred and secular have never remained static. Rather, throughout the ages, forms and functions of worship have continuously been redefined and reshaped. The style that seems to shape today's religious worship climate is a contemporary phenomenon of experiential religious expression.

For instance, John Garraty states that, "In 1790, the religious picture in the United States already showed considerable (and characteristic) variety."[12] And typically, as I stated earlier, these stylistic preferences did not always have, or had little if anything to do with race or ethnicity.

The African American historian, Carter G. Woodson, in his work, *The History of the Negro Church* says, "The Presbyterians, who welcomed the Negroes, moreover, were not much more successful in proselytizing them."[13] In fact, the blacks who did go to the Presbyterian Church in no way showed a desire to adopt the traditional methods and styles of Presbyterian worship. Instead, like their white Methodist and white Baptist counterparts, they preferred a freer, less formal worship style."[14] The point is that the tradition of emotionally expressive, free worship is not exclusively, "a black thing." At least it wasn't in the past. Says Garraty, "It was not unusual at a Methodist meeting for [white] women to faint, [white] men to shout in strange tongues, and the minister himself to windmill his arms and bawl himself red-faced."[15] So, the question of what is or what is not sacred or secular, order or disorder, comely or uncomely, regarding expressions of worship and its practices has been an issue of debate throughout American church history; but, of course, not solely on the basis of race. Some whites, just like blacks, in early American Christianity, did not favor the prim and proper, ritualistic congregational style.

Despite the fact that, in 1803 the Presbyterians did have an outcry against emotionalism exhibited during the camp meetings that were held in Kentucky and Ohio, the General Assembly announced, "God is a God of order and not of confusion, and whatever tends to destroy the comely order of his worship is not from him."[16] Though this rebuke did not inspire a mass exodus as it had with Richard Allen and Absalom Jones with the Methodists in 1777, blacks did not unite in large numbers with the Presbyterian Church. According to Carter G. Woodson, there were ". . . hardly 20,000 Negroes in the Presbyterian Church prior to the Civil War."[17]

In modern society, the secularization of the African American religious experience has been depicted in the media in such television sitcoms as, "Amen," "Good News," and in movies like, Whoopi Goldberg's, "Sister Act," as juvenile, childish, and driven by infantile emotions.

In the mainstream movie, "The Blues Brothers," starring John Belushi and Dan Aykroyd, singer James Brown is featured as an acrobatic preacher who slides across the pulpit, as Dan Aykroyd and John Belushi do back flips down the church aisle. Though Whoopi Goldberg's movie, and that of Aykroyd and Belushi, and even, Eddie Murphy's "Coming to America," are all done in good fun—these movie versions of African American religious experiences are all contributors to the power of stereotyping. Of black church life, these otherwise entertaining depictions are detractions. They add to the cynical perceptions, and the sarcasms about African American religious experiences being anything but able to deliver on the promise of a truly sacred, fulfilling spiritual experience. Television and cinema have been equally successful conveying a picture of white worship experiences as sterile, boring, lifeless and lacking in any outward show of conviction about Christ. Tragically, often these assumptions, [racial] perceptions by blacks and whites about who one another are, what they do in their churches, and how they hold to these ideas as fact, when neither have fully ever worshipped in the "other's" community. And by these behaviors, artificial, subtle yet sustainable lines are drawn between the two groups. And at the same time, the perpetuation of the tradition of separation erases any distinction there is between that which is sacred and that which is secular.

As evidenced by black and white worshippers in America, that which is secular is a neutral safe space. To hear God, to obey God, to humbly submit to His will is daring, but sacred. Unless the epochal distinction of black Christian and white Christian is buried, and with it the racial strife that has permeated the history of the Church in America, the light of Christ's life and the suffering of His cross will continue to be obscured, buried with each service that is gathered in his name. To do anything less would be neither sacred, nor secular; it would be, merely sinful.

NOTES

1. Rudolf Otto, *The Idea of the Holy* (Oxford University Press, London: 1973), 6-7.
2. Emile Durkheim, *The Elementary Forms of Religious Life* (Macmillan Publishing, New York, 1965), 62
3. Michael O. Emerson and Christian Smith, *Divided by Faith: Evangelical Religion and the Problem of Race in America* (Oxford University Press, New York, 2000), 7.

4. Timothy E. Fulop and Albert J. Raboteau, *African-American Religion: Interpretive Essays in History and Culture* (Routledge, New York & London, 1979), 61.

5. Winthrop S. Hudson, *Religion in America: An historical account of the development of American religious life* (Macmillian Publishing, New York, 1987), 133.

6. Robert E. Webber, *Ancient-Future Faith: Rethinking Evangelism for a Postmodern World* (Baker Books, Grand Rapids, Michigan, 2004), 104.

7. Hoyt L.Hickman, *A Primer for Church Worship* (Abingdon Press, Nashville, 1984), 25-26. Hickman served as Assistant General Secretary of the Section on Worship of the Board of Discipleship of the United Method Church, and editor of Abingdon's Supplemental Worship resources series.

8. ————. Hickman, *A Primer for Church Worship*, 26.

9. ————. Hickman, *A Primer for Church Worship*, 26.

10. ————. Hickman, *A Primer for Church Worship*, 27.

11. ————. James F. White, *Protestant Worship: Traditions in Transition* (Westminster/John Knox Press: Louisville, Kentucky, 1985), 205.

12. John A. Garraty, ed. Historical Viewpoint: Notable Articles from American Heritage, Third Edition, Volume One to 1877 (Harper & Row, New York, 1979), 242.

13. Carter G. Woodson, *The History of the Negro Church* (The Associated Publishers, Association for the Study of Negro Life and History, Washington, D.C. 1921), 84.

14. ————. Woodson, *The History of the Negro Church*, 84.

15. ————. Garraty, ed. Historical Viewpoint: Notable Articles from American Heritage, Third Edition, Volume One to 1877, 245.

16. ————. Hudson, Religion in America, 133.

17. ————. Woodson, The History of the Negro Church, 84.

Chapter Five

The High Cost of Reconciliation

There is no sound or theological reasons that from across the spectrum of Christianity, worship experiences cannot be shared routinely by interracial congregants. Regardless of the forms or expressions that mark or typify how people worship, there should always be a welcoming arm to others to share that experience. However, the cost of reconciliation would be high and worthy of the high cost of Christ's sacrifice if Christian adherents would work to close the gulf of separation and racism. If, in fact, Jesus Christ is at the center of all Christian events; then in everything that is done in His name, Christians should be able to—in spirit and in truth, reconcile Jesus around His own name. And a major aspiration of that reconciliation must be "unity of the spirit in the bond of peace."

But the bond of peace is too often a far cry from the majority of religious experiences. How people express themselves religiously, and their fierce adherence to their own unique tenets is under girding catastrophes that are playing out worldwide. The reason for this is that the essence of any religious experience occurs within a social context, in the world in which people live, work and worship. Likewise, Christian theology does not happen in a vacuum. Even though most people who claim to be Christian know what it means to be a Christian—a follower of Christ, i.e., love for all of humanity, humility, peace, sacrifice for others, a lack of condescension toward others not like oneself— many limit their abandonment, if any all, to the principles Christ taught. The products of such lack of abandon to the actual teachings of Christ are marginal Christians who have a marginal knowledge of His word and works. Simply put, people love or they do not love, they are either united or they are divided.

Furthermore, the separation of Christian worshippers on the basis of race and ethnicity reflects a misrepresentation or a distortion of the Christian message. It is a misrepresentation of the Christian theology that seeks to support the message of unity and brotherhood. Social evidence clearly supports the idea that "tradition" rather than "theology" aligns itself with the separation of blacks and whites from intentional shared worship.

In 1999, The Barna Research Group conducted a study that concluded, "As for commitment to Christianity, the survey data show that it may be more American than ethnic to associate but have a lukewarm commitment to the faith. Blacks and whites reflect similar commitment profiles. . ." "Americans are not completely engaged with their faith, regardless of their ethnic background.[1]

According to Rick Warren in his important work, The Purpose Driven Church, "The goal of a tradition-driven church is simply to perpetuate the past. Change is almost always seen as negative, and stagnation is interpreted as stability."[2] White churches and black churches have been, over the centuries of their operation in America, baptized into a mystical world of tradition. Each church has its "written in stone" rituals, its traditions that have withstood the test of time and use; consequently, the winds of change are threatening. Tradition, therefore, evokes the adage over and over again, "This is the way we have always done things, why do we have to do them differently?"

Under the umbrella of this attitude, it is unlikely that either side will be dislodged anytime in the near future from the way that things are done. Barna's research, indeed, reveals that the status quo may continue since, "older generations—Seniors, Builders, and Boomers—have traditionally been resistant to these changes [of inclusiveness]. We cannot expect to influence our community for good until we repent of racist attitudes, inaccurate assumptions, and unrealistic expectations related to racial diversity."[3] The question which follows is can or will the Church of Jesus Christ break down these seemingly impervious walls of racial separation and move forward with the real work of the Lord.

Decades ago, Dr. King stated, "There is little hope for us until we become tough-minded enough to break loose from the shackles of prejudice, half-truths, and downright ignorance."[4] A generation later, little has actually changed regarding the spiritual infrastructure of the American Christian Church. Dr. King's daughter, Reverend Bernice King is still preaching the same message of longing for change, and with the same intensity as her father. When she says, ". . . we don't deal with this race issue, and we don't preach enough about it. I believe God is disturbed and hurt by that,"[5] she is echoing the same urgency of her late father, that Christian churches must become communities. According to Louis A. Drummond, "Evangelist Billy Graham's stance on racism, particularly during the turbulent era of the 1950s, also bore fruit. In all these racial upheavals, Graham kept to his basic philosophy, saying, 'We are ultimately not going to solve the race problems in America until men truly love each other.'"[6]

In my own unscientific, but revealing experiment with students from predominately white colleges to determine how they felt about and would respond to interracial worship experiences, my findings were eye-opening to say the least. In 1991, I dispatched a large number of both black and white students to try out, for the first time, a worship service outside their own traditional experience. Included in this group were students from Ohio, Kentucky, Indiana and mid-western states. There were also a few students in residence from Saudi Arabia and Japan who also took part in the experiment. Participants ranged in ages from eighteen to forty-five years old and represented a cross-section of culture, social, economic and religious worship experiences.

A large number of the white students, who participated for the first-time in an African American church service said that their contact with the tradition was, "fun," "awesome," "wild," "exciting," "a celebration," "like the movie, Sister Act with Whoopi Goldberg." One student stated, ["It was] the first time I danced in church." Another said the music was "like a band playing for the Lord."[7] It was interesting to me that these responses corresponded to a secularized expectation of what a black worship experience would deliver based on entertainment and performance rather than spiritual worship. These statements conveyed preconceived notions that are steeped in age old stereotypes of black churches and what goes on in them. In fact, one student was disappointed, let down because his own experience was not like the ones of the students who made these statements. He said, "I thought there would be more people at the service than there were. I also thought there would be a lot more clapping and dancing around than there was the day I went."[8] Another said, "I am glad that it was required because it left a lasting impression on me. Such a lasting impression that I brought my mom the next week, and she thoroughly enjoyed it as well."[9]

Another white female student said of her first visit to an African American church, ". . . it felt strange to be a minority in an all black environment. I felt self-conscious . . . it was like we had a different God."[10] Sent to an all white congregation, an African American male returned to say, "I found the church welcoming. However, it was a non-traditional, very charismatic church."[11] He also offered this opinion, "I believe that some black people are afraid to have whites come to their churches for fear the whites will take over." [12] A white female expressed a similar opinion; black churches offer blacks "an opportunity to rejoice in the Lord without the presence of whites and it is the freedom of African Americans to separate their lives from whites for one plus hours each week— whites would be "overwhelming" or "dominating" in the black church."

This exercise changed the way many of the non African American students perceived the black church. One white student enjoyed the black worship service so much she thought it exceeded the services at her own church: "I have visited many Protestant, Catholic and Unitarian Churches in my search for spirituality. In most of the church services I have witnessed, the spirit becomes lost in rituals. So much emphasis is often put on following the strict guidelines of ceremony the meaning of the ceremony becomes secondary. On the contrary, the [black] church service I attended was with genuine love and appreciation for Jesus Christ."[13]

As alternative for many of the black students who came from a more formal tradition such as Catholic or Episcopalian churches, they found, when attending white churches with a similar liturgy, the worship was the same. One black student said, "I see the similarities in how we conduct services. One time I was flipping the channels and watched a bit of a white church performed their morning services and they were identical to our church, even sounded like them. . ."[14]

It goes without saying: everyone of the students learned something about the interplay of "power and meaning" in worship from the congregation they attended. At least one student learned that the black worship experience isn't monolithic, that it isn't guaranteed to deliver the stereotypical performance of worship—though how disappointing that may have been for him.

For my students, this experimental study could have been a life changing experience. It might have enhanced their lives as a spiritual epiphany; except the encounter came short of making a lasting impression on all of them as none expressed any interest in continuing to visit the churches they went to worship: "it was just a black or white church visitation." Even though they found familiar experiences, or new and pleasing experiences at the respective churches of their visit, they all continued to look at church going along racial lines.

There was another interesting discovery. Despite the opportunity of going to their assigned churches without incident, many came back to me to ask whether I thought they might be welcomed as "others" in the various church communities. Obviously, there remained that over-arching pale of racism affecting the incidents of the student visits. To me, such questions were like having brothers and sisters of the same family ask permission to enter their father's house. Unfortunately, one of the tentacles of this very painful manifestation of what amounts to a deep spiritual struggle in Christ's church is the "fight over control," place, meaning and power.

The concern isn't out of the ordinary. The threat of change complicates the hierarchy of authority within both the black and the white church in the way that both communities have understood it for centuries. These two important church communities are splendid posters of study for any one wishing to examine the difference between what it means to desegregate and integrate. With this picture, "It is more accurate to say that the vast majority of black Americans and white Americans simply coexist in separate realms, interacting when necessary and occasionally crossing over but ultimately retreating to our different worlds."[15]

According to Benjamin E. Mays, and Joseph W. Nicholson, in their early work, *The Negro Church*, the genius of the black church was the opportunity the church gave to common laborers and domestics an ability to transform their "nobodiness" into "sombodiness."[16] For example, the local school janitor during the week could on Sunday morning become chairman of the deacon board directing the affairs of the church with pride and authority. The black woman, who is the nanny during the week, could on Sunday morning become the president of the missionary circle, possessing a tremendous amount of influence and authority in the church. St. Clair Drake and Horace Clayton describe this kind of reductionist perspective as the compensatory model, a way in which blacks were able to overcome the oppressive conditions of daily life. The [black] church's main attraction is the opportunity it gives for large masses of people to function in an organized group, to compete for prestige, to be elected to office, to exercise power and control, to win applause and acclaim."[17]

Interestingly, though Drake and Clayton's work focused primarily on the black church of the sixties, this model could very well apply to any church regardless of racial or ethnic affiliation. While on the one hand this appears to be a positive attribute of the church, the down side, of course, occurs when certain standards of spiritual or organizational excellence are not required for those persons seeking to exercise power and control over others and the affairs of the institution.

Because of the socio-economic conditions at the end of the 20th century and now into the 21st century, the compensatory model remains a factor in the life of the black church, so much so that it trumps the life of Christ and the demands of Christian orthodoxy for far too many blacks. While there has been continuous growth of the black middle class, Henry Louis Gates, Jr. said that, ". . . swelling ranks of the black poor, a category that (like the black middle class) now encompasses about a third of black families."[18] As such, a disproportionate number of blacks in America still lag behind in every predictor of a quality life and see themselves as oppressed. For these, the black church continues to provide a safe haven and continues to compensate for those feelings of disenfranchisement and "lostness" in a society that breads fertile ground for them to feel like "nobody." Withstanding the inevitable internal struggles for power within the black church, in many respects it is still the place where blacks feel they belong. In the black church, worshipers are able

to gather hope and feel like they are important. The black church has historically been a small quite sphere within a large hostile one. There is great and
encouraging evidence, however, that the black church in some arenas have a
more expansive view of the world, of itself, of its place in it; subsequently, its
members have a more expansive and progressive view of themselves and
their potential in the larger society.

Needless to say, the white church does and has always provided a similar
safe haven of empowerment for its members. As well, it provides them with
a safe cover from the intrusion of outside cultural tenets it does not want to
involve in its worship venues. In light of these deeply rooted control issues,
one can only speculate about what a racially shared community might ini-
tially look like. For instance, how would a racially merged church share the
power between a leading white deacon and a leading black deacon? How
would the lead duties of the missionary circle be parsed between a strong
willed black sister and that of an equally strong willed white one? How comfortable would a white church be with a black treasurer in "control" of the
churches' finances? Would the black church be comfortable with a white
clerk recording the history of their church events and vice-versa? Also, would
a gifted black worship leader be ready to cede leadership to a white worship
leader just as, or more gifted? Would long metered hymns popularized in the
black church borne of experiences of its soul be tolerated by white congregants who are accustomed to music that may be more or less ingrained in their
spiritual history, but of things gone through quite different?

Clearly the questions are numerous and could be conjectured ad infini-
tum. I know that there are no easy or clear cut answers, for there is no monolithic or "one size fits all" church community. Yet these are just the elementary issues of what obstacles might have to be overcome if blacks and
whites were ever to try to cross the divide of individualism and racism to
unify and to clarify the generally accepted assumptions and myths that char-
acterize elements of both the black and the white church. In spite of any obstacle, the task of overcoming needs to begin. In the words of L. Venchal
Booth, founder of the Progressive National Baptist Convention, when
speaking of the American Church, he wrote, "The white church needs to become more black and the black church needs to become more white. That's
the simple way to put it."[19]

NOTES

1. George Barna, *The Second Coming of the Church* (Word Publishing, Nashville,
1998), 3.

2. Rick Warren, *The Purpose Driven Church* (Zondervan Publishing House, Grand Rapids, MI, 1995), 77.

3. Barna, *The Second Coming of the Church*, 53.

4. Martin Luther King, Jr. James M. Washington, ed. *Testament of Hope: The Essential Writings and Speeches of Martin Luther King, Jr.* (San Francisco, Harper Collins, 1991), 218.

5. Carol Stream, Interview with Reverend Dr. Bernice King. "She has a dream, too." Christianity Today (June 16, 1997), 36.

6. Lewis A. Drummond, *The Evangelist* (Word Publishing, Nashville, Tennessee, 2001), 86.

7. Terriel R. Byrd, *Non-African American Perception of the African American Religious Experience: How that Perception Impacts 11:00 Sunday Morning Being the Most Segregated Hour in American Life* (UMI Dissertation Services, Ann Arbor, Michigan, 1999), 25.

8. Byrd, *Non African American Perception,* 121.

9. Byrd, *Non African American Perception*, 122.

10. Byrd, Dissertation, appendices.

11. Byrd, Dissertation, appendices.

12. Byrd, Dissertation, appendices.

13. Byrd, *Non African American Perception*, 125.

14. Byrd, *Non African American Perception,* 122.

15. Martin Luther King, Jr. *Where Do We Go From Here: Chaos or Community?* (Harper & Row Publishers, New York, Evanston, 1967), 109.

16. Benjamin E. Mays and Joseph W. Nicholson, *The Negro's Church* (New York: Institute of Religious Research, 1933), 278.

17. Hart M. Nelsen and Anne Kusener Nelsen, *Black Church in the Sixties*, (University Press, Lexington, Kentucky, 1975), 9.

18. Henry Louis Gates, Jr. and Cornel West, *The Future of the Race* (Vintage Books, NY, 1996), 24.

19. Edward Gilreath, associate ed. "The Forgotten Founder, Christianity Today" (March 2002): 68.

Chapter Six

The Fanciful Interplay
of Color and Culture

For many centuries, the social stratification of color and culture in America kept both blacks and whites in their places. Nonetheless, today, the Church finds itself at the dawn of a new century, with the progress of race relations in every sector of American society at a stand still. Not much is being done on a national level with the same impetus of the Civil Rights Movement to continue the work of integration and reconciliation. Everyone knows that there is still a deeply ingrained racial problem here that needs to be addressed honestly—to the roots of its painful genesis, if this nation is ever going to be as welcoming to people of all races, ethnicities, and national backgrounds as it says it is. If it chose to, the Church could become a powerful broker of deep reconciliation in this country if it can ever see itself outside the strict boundaries of the past, and function in a new spiritual and social truth.

When both black and white Christian communities begin to exclude from their hearts and minds, the reasons of the Church divide, they may then begin to look to serious engagement for reconciliation, but not until they heal the historical reality that race has played in the negative construction of church theology and tradition. The fact that color delineations and identifications are still actualities in America does not excuse the continued existence of the same dispositions and attitudes in the Church. The Body of the Church has to begin to act like and look like its Head; that is, if it is to carry out the Great Commission of Jesus Christ to go into the entire world and preach the Gospel.

In order to achieve this ideal, though, America must not seek to become a color blind society. Too much is at risk if it does so. Rather, the optimal course would be for it to appreciate its great diversity and the dynamism brought to it by the various cultures that now populate the country. The Church is the

most natural entity to make this happen, and must lead the way. Michael Eric
Dyson states that,

> The ideal of a color blind society is a pale imitation of a greater, grander ideal:
> of living in a society where our color won't be denigrated, where our skin will
> be neither a badge for undue privilege nor a sign of social stigma. Because skin,
> race, and color have in the past been the basis for social inequality, they must
> play a role in righting the social wrongs on which our society was built.[1]

To continue in social myopia is to go on pretending that America is not a
country made of diverse communities; it is to continue to ignore the fundamental basis of its existence. To a certain extent, most American institutions,
only forced to do so by the law, have moved toward some level of integration.
To this day, in some cases, the numbers of minorities that participate in large
public companies and educational institutions appear to be "tokenism." To the
significant degree that race matters in America, the society has lumbered
through one of the numerous layers of racism and inequity to a superficial tolerance of itself. This is better than nothing, better than what it was before, but
it isn't enough. In as much as this passage has permitted a new kind of civility
in social interactions in education and better economic opportunities for everyone, it is a magnificent prelude to what could ultimately be a country where
civic, social and economic parity is universal. But as a nation, we have too long
rested on our laurels. The Church can pick up the blood stained banner of racial
justice, to pursue harmony, and continue the march toward the mark of the high
call of God in Christ Jesus by ensuring that America is a hostile society to no
one. Author Shelby Steele says that, "Integration has become an abstract term
today, having to do with little more than numbers and racial balances. Race is
a separate reality in American Society, an entity that carries its own potential for
power, a mark of fate that class can soften considerably but not eradicate."[2]

The seemingly intractable issue of race separation in the Church is per-
plexing. Of course, if asked, neither blacks nor whites would readily admit in
this day and age that color is what keeps them apart. More willingly, both
groups would say, it is more about choice and familiarity than it is about
color. Neither group, blacks or whites, would admit to what Shelby Steele describes as "race holding" or, the false security gained by not moving beyond
one's own ethnic group. Further, most blacks and whites are much more at
ease discussing the culture divide than they are talking about the color divide,
though we continue to classify ourselves into color groupings easily as it regards the: "black church" and the "white church."

Culture, however, may point to something beyond religious experience within
the scope of an institution. Martin E. Marty writes that culture, "represents

everything that humans do to and make of nature. Since humans work in concert, band together, come as families and clans and tribes and nations, they also merit consideration in "multi's" in "multicultural." If within a religious culture there is valuation or devaluation of a particular religious practice as being acceptable and the other unacceptable, might not that hinder one from sharing more fully in another's cultural experience? Why of course. The perceptions made by white and black worshippers speak to what each group values or does not value culturally. This too reveals what Paul Tillich says: "Religion as ultimate concern is the meaning-giving substance of culture, and culture is the totality of forms in which the basic concern of religion expresses itself. In abbreviation: religion is the substance of culture, and culture is the form of religion."[3] It is fair to say, that this idea, which apparently supersedes the word of God "to be one as we are One" (St. John 17:21), this concept of culture over the Gospel reveals there is much heart work to be done by all Christians.

Interestingly, the ambiguous nature of ethnic cultures in America makes it more acceptable and less offensive in meandering through the maze of utter confusion as it relates to the Christian Church in America. ". . . black and white culture in their various forms have a powerful pull on their own constituencies . . . But choice and culture are not always the determining factors. Plain old prejudice is also part of the mix," according to Stienhorn and Diggs-Brown.

This may be true, but it still perplexes, though, that the Church has exhibited no desire to mirror the socio-political arena regarding desegregating the country. Neither blacks nor whites should feel comfortable with appearing too comfortable in segregated churches. If blacks and whites are comfortable enough at work together, sometimes side by side in swank offices, and on factory floors; they shop side by side in grocery stores and in malls, they yell and scream together at sports events for their children and for professional athletes, they go to company picnics and parties together, and for decades now, eat in the same restaurants, the Church has to also lift itself above its tunnel vision and move forward. In other words, there ought to be a spiritual plane, on which compromise can occur, on the part of both communities, that is comfortable enough to facilitate one another's presence together in the same church sanctuaries for the sake of God, the Heavenly Father.

The work of Leonard Steinhorn and Barbara Diggs- Brown highlights this lamentable issue: "We are one of the most religious countries in the western world, yet in this nation of regular churchgoers, most blacks and most whites pray separately to the same God. Even as we transcend the temporal, we remain earthly bound by the color line that holds us."[4] The separation of the religious communities is not merely an isolated event, but it is an ongoing aberration.

When Dr. King was alive, the condition of the churches concerned him deeply. He said, "The churches are called upon to recognize the urgent necessity of taking a forthright stand on this [ending of practices of racism] crucial issue. If we are to remain true to the gospel of Jesus Christ, we cannot rest until segregation and discrimination is banished from every corner of American life. Even though morality may not be legislated, behavior can be regulated. . . We need religion and education to change attitudes and to change the hearts of men"[5] In his words, "segregation in the Christian Church is the most tragic form of segregation because it is a blatant denial that we are all one in Christ."[6] Characteristically, his hope was that the Church would wake itself, because the achievement of a just and equitable society rested partially in the vision of a Church vitally awake to its social responsibilities.

The fundamental crisis of racism has roots in America that have had 230 years to imbed themselves into the American way of life. Implicit in cultural delineation is the assumption that there is reason, based on natural differences, for blacks and whites to separate — that they are, in fact, so different their cultures prohibit shared participation in worship services. This is erroneous thinking, but it is so much a part of the way we have always thought about race and culture that it is what is accepted as part of the American way of thinking. For all intents and purposes of progress, it needs to be gotten out of the way.

Certainly, salvation, the finished work of Christ is more important than culture or color. If blacks and whites can begin to see themselves as the fascination and ingenuity of God's divine love, prerogative and handiwork, then maybe as well we will get over the centuries of taking ourselves, our cultures and the color of our skin so seriously. Maybe then we could get on with His work.

Thankfully, the Charismatic Movement continues to lead the way in cultural synchronization of worship. Habitually, blacks, whites, Hispanics and Asians gather in centers around the country at various times every week. Most often, these services have a free wheeling atmosphere in which all participants, regardless of cultural background engage in services that are spirited, emotional and deeply Pentecostal in the way they are conducted; in the way adherents express themselves. In this atmosphere, where everyone believes at these high emotional times, the Spirit of God is present, these participants tend to identify more with one another as Charismatic Christians [brothers and sisters in the Lord] than they do with themselves as members of a particular race or culture.

It is encouraging to witness this kind of cultural amalgamation in the Church; yet there is one disquieting disparity. In a large number of these Charismatic Churches, unless the pastor is black, there is little or no black, or other ethnic leadership present. If the pastor is black, there will be few if any white parishioners in these independent [many led by a family hub] churches. On the other hand, in white Charismatic Churches, there are a large and growing number of the followers who are black; despite the fact there is little black if any, or any ethnic representation in the leadership of these communities. It seems that black worshippers are more comfortable going to white churches with all white leadership, than whites are going and placing themselves under all black leadership.

Again, it is this perception born of fear, and the unwillingness of there to be even an attempt to cross the bridge to allay, in an authentic way, these fears that shape "power and meaning" in religious communities; that keep the various groups of Christians apart and isolated from one another.

In events recorded at the National Conference of Black Christians, James Cone challenged the mainstream Christian Church with his theology, and voiced his frustrations and his views in 1969,

> that blackness, justice and power were not antithetical to the Christian faith. We are unalterably committed to the effecting of a more equitable power balance 'by whatever means are necessary.' Means additional to negotiation are now necessary. The time has come for us to resort to the use of unusual forms of pressure upon the white church structure if we are to realize the legitimate goal of a literal transfer of power.[7]

The Church seems an unlikely place for a power struggle, but they do happen—in all black churches, in all white churches, and in churches and Christian organizations where blacks perceive themselves to be present, but underrepresented; or where their concerns and interests are submerged under those of the majority and are never heard and acted upon.

Such perceptions of insensitivity led to the highly publicized split of Father George A. Stallings, Jr., an African American priest, from the Roman Catholic Church. In an interview with Emerge Magazine in April 1995, Father Stallings was asked, "Was there any specific factor that caused you to leave the Roman Catholic Church?" He responded this way:

> Oh yes, it's all tied to racism. The distorted, pathological thinking that White people, particularly White males have that they are better than any other race or group of people, and that they have the right—the sole right—to dictate what is best for people that they don't even understand, and then will not allow those racial or ethnic groups to exercise decisions over their own lives to create a kind of religious expression that ministers to their profound spiritual and cultural needs.[8]

Although Father Stallings is a member of the Catholic Church, his concerns mirror those of many black and ethnic worshippers who do seek to merge their religious experiences with those of other cultures. Nevertheless, to break away and create yet another schism along racial lines in the church is not the way to enter into an effective dialogue that would eliminate the need for Christians to break ranks with one another for safe places to worship and express themselves. This is not constructive and to resort to this measure and others that create spiritual fault lines is the action that led to Dr. King calling 11:00 o'clock Sunday morning the most segregated hour in America.

In order to reach accords of understanding, blacks and whites have to become more sophisticated in their thinking about one another. As Christians, neither can afford to rely on the simplistic impressions that typify their thinking about each other. Racism is much more complex and difficult than cursory thinking will permit to uncover assessable avenues to solutions to it. According to Michael Eric Dyson, in Race Rules: Navigating the Color Line, referring to the 1960's, "I'm not suggesting that blacks and whites agreed about what each group saw as the source of racial conflict. In fact, like today, they often didn't agree about what they saw, many whites saw roses where blacks saw thorns.... race is complex and choked with half-discarded symbols and muddied signs — our skills of interpretation have to be more keen, our reading more nuanced"[9]

Researchers Steinhorn and Diggs-Brown have a more poignant view of the cost and outlook for integration of white and black worshipers: "Blacks may be more willing to accept these conditions because to them integration is a net gain. But because most whites don't want integration or believe they gain little from it beyond their self congratulatory acceptance of the ideal, they have little interest in accepting the sacrifice."[10]

These excellent scholars make a compelling argument regarding the acceptance of net gains and losses on the ideal of integration; yet, I must counter with the proposal that the motivation of both parties is nothing more than power drives. For the most part, black Christians are no more eager to integrate with white churches than are whites with black churches. If what one means by integration is that blacks unite with white churches, I refer to the comments of Pastor Charles Lyons of Armitage Baptist Church [a multiracial church] in Chicago. He commented to Christianity Today by saying, "It's about more than just mixing races. I wince every time I hear that line, '11:00 o'clock Sunday morning is the most segregated hour in America.' Give me a break! You couldn't drag most black people to most white churches."[11]

Pastor Lyons likely sees the separation as valid based on cultural grounds. Conversely, I believe the codification of cultural elements has in fact empowered the black church institutionally. After many years of discrimination directed toward blacks in America and the glaring perceptions of inferiority assumed through stereotypical conditioning, the black church now takes pride in its unique cultural forms and socio-economic empowerment agenda.

Unfortunately, these are the very issues: self-empowerment and culture, which may hinder both black and white churchgoers from effective engagement in efforts that lead to integration. Thus, it is very unlikely that any meaningful transformation toward integration will occur at the powerful convention level. One can only look at the battles fought within the ranks of black and white mainstream denominational conventions from the past and the present to see that if the status quo is embraced, not much will ever change. Many of the battles have been either fought over the acquiring of positions within the convention or divisions over ideological differences, which tends to draw lines in the "theological sands" of conservatism and liberalism. Attention given to these issues provide little room for serious discussion of integration and the balance of power between blacks and whites within the Christian conventions on the basis of Biblical understanding of the call and mission of the unified Church.

The Church like any family unit is a very intimate place. It is often in the church where relationships are solidified, friendships are nurtured and sustained. The Sunday school class or Bible study gatherings become places where people discuss and grapple over some of their most personal moral issues, and matters regarding marriage and family, obedience and sacrifice. It is a sacred space in that it allows people who belong to a familiar group to share and embrace on the deepest levels of confession and intimacy. There they play and pray together as members of a family. Regardless of where the church is today spiritually, these attributes make it more than a social institution; it transcends the boundaries of the market place. In that regard, the black church and the white church have to be respected for the haven it provides for its worshippers.

The very nature of the color-identifying label classifications within American Christianity is laced with subtle reminders of perceived differences of inequality by blacks and/or feelings of indifference or superiority by whites. The early church had its battles too—those that had to do with the propagation of the Gospel, the Apostles and other disciples eventually settled among themselves. Those that had to do with race, class and gender, God settled those for them: 'Call not that which I have created unclean.' Lazarus was raised from the dead; and the woman who was caught in adultery was told to "go and sin no more." There remains a place in God where the church communities can go together in God. It is a place where He can command greater blessings upon them.

NOTES

1. Michael Eric Dyson, *Race Rules: Navigating the Color Line*, (Random House, New York, 1997), 224.

2. Shelby Steele, *The Content of our Character: A New Vision of Race in America,* (Harper Perennial/Harper Collins Publishers, New York, NY, 1990), 148.

3. Paul Tillich, *Theology of Culture,* (Oxford University Press, Oxford, London, 1970), 42.

4. Leonard Steinhorn and Barbara Diggs Brown, *By the Color of our Skin: The Illusion of Integration and The Reality of Race*, (A Plume Book, New York, 1992), 62.

5. Martin Luther King, Jr. *A Testament of Hope: The Essential Writings and Speeches of Martin Luther King, Jr.* (HarperCollins, New York, 1991), 89, 213.

6. Lewis Baldwin, There is a Balm in Gilead: The Cultural Roots of Dr. Martin Luther King, Jr. (Fortress Press, Minneapolis, MN 1991), 51.

7. James H. Cone, For My People: Black Theology the Black Church? (Orbis Books, Mary Knoll, New York 1984), 11.

8. George A. Stallings, "Renegade Priest," Emerge Magazine, Volume 6 (April 1995,): 22, 23.

9. Michael Eric Dyson, *Race Rules: Navigating the Color Line* (Vintage Books, New York, 1996), 25.

10. Steinhorn and Diggs-Brown, *By the Color of our Skin*, 222.

11. Pastor Charles Lyons, "CT Forum, Divided by Faith interview", Christianity Today, (October 2, 2000), 44.

Chapter Seven

The Layers of Meaning
Found in Religious Worldviews

The authentic message of Christ transcends any one religion and any one worldview. The difficulties that shaped the Christian religious worldview in America, as has been discussed throughout this work, can be easily traced to the events of a sacred, but wounded past. Deep and intractable meaning can be ascribed to religious worship that is only to be understood within the context of the worldview that has shaped it. As Eugene Genovese states, in one instance, that, "the spiritual experience of the slaves took shape as part of a tradition emanating from Africa . . . It is no overstatement to say that religion is not just one complex of African culture, but the catalyst of the complex . . . . Religion was an aspect, not a feature of society—the vital way in which the entire human body collectively expressed its essences."[1] In other words, early periods of subjugation and dehumanization gave rise to the unique expressions that typify the African American tradition of worship, which, though practiced throughout the ages in America, has its deepest roots in African expressionism.

Concomitantly, Europeans who took to the dangerous high seas for religious freedom fled Amsterdam, Holland for America in the seventeenth century to pursue the freedom to worship as they wished. Their quest gave rise to a deep sense of mission and Manifest Destiny that superimposed itself on everything else they did after arriving to America. They, as did the Africans, who were forging a new way of worship, saw religion as all encompassing. The Africans saw religion as part and parcel of their survival; the Europeans felt that religion should be the bedrock of every part of civic and everyday life. And in its earliest expressions, these nascent American worshipers sought to include everyone; including the Africans, in their religious hub. The center of that spirit of inclusiveness that Europeans tried to promote, however, did not hold. It began to bifurcate as people who wanted to be free from religion sought to be so, as well as with denominationalism, of course, also came major church divergence that seemed to support the eventual separation of whites and blacks in the same worship assemblies.

With such changes, the texturing of the American religious landscape moved forward. Obviously, people began to create and adhere to their own tenets and views to the exclusion of any others. These religious traditions and worldviews were and still are infused with meaning that includes diversity and varying styles and practices of worship.

For example, whether it is a Baptist, Methodist or Pentecostal worshiper who says, "We really had church this morning," it signals a depth and layer of meaning that, perhaps, can only be understood by those of the group or by the person or persons who uttered the comment. What can be clearly understood is this: whether Baptist, Methodist, or Pentecostal, the statement signals something happening on a deeper level, something beyond the visible, beyond the clapping of the hands, the shouting, or the rapping of the feet on the floors of church buildings. What may be even clearer in the uniqueness of such a seemingly innocuous statement in response to worship is that there is the inherent blocking of consensus about whom or what Christianity is really all about. On the surface and below it, close affiliation with a particular religious worldview suggests spiritual absoluteness most Christians never venture to examine; ever, hardly, with a mind to change.

Yet, the entire concept of Christ's message of obedience to God involves change; examination and reexamination of one's own heart and motives; the ability to change, the willingness of continuous inner change.

The change of which I write and speak is not simply change for the sake of change, it is change which challenges and shakes up the status quo. Part of the veneer of religious devotion is couched in the exclusivity of the branches and ethnic diversities of American Christianity. The function of said exclusivity has served so often as a perfect platform from which Christians make accusations against one another; to find differences that are strong enough to serve as ongoing barriers of separation. An example of Christ's call to deep change, and a move away from such artificial differences, is exemplified in His relationship to the Scribes and Pharisees, the religious movers and framers of thought and doctrine of His time. A notable interaction occurred between these men and Christ when He defended the woman caught in adultery. As follows,

They said to him, "Teacher, this woman was caught in the very act of committing adultery. Now in the law Moses commanded us to stone such women. What do you say? They said this to test him, so that they might have some charge to bring against him. Jesus bent down and wrote with his finger on the ground (John 8:4-6).[2]

Plainly, from this important tract of history, it is clear that the way the Lord dealt with the religious structure in His time was, too say the least, unsettling. He started by shaking up that accepted establishment. The actions he took and the things he did and taught were aimed at dislodging the strongholds of tradition and the doctrines of men; His discourse, in word and in deed, were intended to bring liberation to people who were weighed down with religious tradition. His teachings and the miracles He performed sought to inspire alternatives to the core tenets of the dead weights of religion—a worldview which did not engage or touch the wounded hearts of men. He only, and not religion and tradition, engaged the hearts of those who were touched by the intervention of His impulse to liberate the human heart and spirit to search for and to know the true life of God: ". . . Woman, where are they? Has no one condemned you?" She said, "No one, sir." And Jesus said, "Neither do I condemn you. Go your way, and from now on do not sin again." (John 8:10, 11).[3]

For me to say that the religious status quo was a killing proposition when Christ walked the earth is an understatement; withstanding, that today, no one in any Christian church would be physically stoned for adultery. But it would not be an overstatement for me to say that there are, in the Church today, in practice and in deed, the equivalents of the same lethal accusations and structural tenets of abandonment. As practiced by today's contemporary Christians, they provide the same kind of spiritual isolation against "the other" or "the outsider" or the "one caught or fallen" in a community like the one this woman experienced. Because of her isolation, and because of the rituals of tradition and culture, she nearly lost her life. Racial isolationism is a ritualistic custom that promotes religious exclusivity and has its own toxic and unwholesome consequences. In the same mood of the Scribes and Pharisees of ancient times, the refusal to relinquish traditions and practices held as sacred by the 21st century Church is the status quo that prevents deep spiritual healing and the metamorphic cleansing of its members.

When I was a young boy of about fourteen, no more, I remember the presence of old Deacon Berry in my church. At the time, he might have been nearing eighty years old. He had some difficulty talking above a whisper due to the fact that he had spent a number of years working in a Virginia coal mine. The effects of the coal dust on his lungs were quite obvious. He spoke in a low throaty baritone that rattled as he talked. Nonetheless, when he reached back at particular times to find one of those long metered hymns, traditional in many African American churches, they were the sorrow songs reminiscent of a distant slave past. He bellowed, seemingly effortlessly: the words, "Father I stretch my hand to thee, no other help I know/ If I would withdraw myself from thee, wither would I go. . ."[4] In these words were a question and an answer. Deacon Berry could easily identity with the struggles of the past while at the same time embracing his faith for what remained of his future and his desire to work to overcome any present difficulties.

Every person in the church, young and old, knew what it meant to an elder who pulled one of those old songs from the private regions of the soul's heartbreaks. The freedom of this old man to plunder his own heart's history and social legacy to do this was about as sacred to him as was the place where he sat; where he was allowed to freely go forth. Would he have been, or anyone like him, or anyone today, ever be allowed to do this in a shared religious environment? The progresses toward this possibility do not look promising. The fears of that which is different, threats of the unknown, the daunting racial history of the country and the Church continue to prevail.

Unfortunately, racial stereotyping and social and cultural conditioning have so influenced black and white churchgoers that any attempt to inject a dose of communal solidarity is met with cynicism, indifference, suspicion or outright distrust and rejection by both groups. On the one hand, whites sometimes view the black church and its role in black life as important and significant, yet as insignificant where it concerns any real contributions to be made to mainstream religious life and culture. Meanwhile, when asked about the impact of slavery on modern black life, the late Dr. John Hope Franklin stated:

> It is both a historical fact and a very powerful force that casts a shadow over the present. When you talk about the role of slavery, ask why do people look at me and think that I'm their servant? What the hell is that all about? If they haven't somehow come to the conclusion that I'm here to serve them the way that my ancestors 150 years ago were there to serve theirs. Imagine asking an 82-year old man to fetch anything for them? Or to serve them, to get their coat or their car or to call me "boy." That's the shadow that's over this whole thing.[5]

On the other hand: Early American Protestants Americanized Christianity in such a way, they also made their expressions and practices uniquely their own through what is considered a Neoplatonistic Christian worldview. Whites appropriated and adapted worship patterns that fit with their new and different environment. A form of "frontier worship characterized by a spirit of immediacy, and little attention was given to tradition and the past"[6] began to be typical. For the sake of building alliances and creating a platform of tolerance and reconciliation, how many blacks are there willing to go to a white church, and would venture routinely into the liturgical quietness and the sometimes precise sterility of a white church service? Apparently, with so many absolutes passed down through time and tradition, both worldviews are closed at this juncture in American Church history, so much so that these traditions cannot be breached in order to heal the breach of separation. Actually, there appears no pliable opening for alteration, change, or sincere arbitration. With these critical outlooks, and the narrowing of thought prevalent on both sides, the historical and racial causes of the separation between black and white worshippers are never given attention and heartfelt validation. Any consideration on whether it is pertinent to mount dialogues that could lead to the disintegration of barriers between the two worship groups go, uncomfortably, unexplored.

Preaching is another anchor tradition in the black church: there are times when the preacher might begin move the sermon to its climatic close—there is the familiar swaying to the call—and the response is: "Go ahead, preach it, and say it." All present know that the end is really the beginning for any black preacher worth his robes. He concludes the sermon, no matter how homiletically precise, or rhythmically accurate, by taking Jesus to the Cross, yet one more time. Some of this is sincere inward, outward, upward worship in gratitude to God for the sacrifice of the life of His son. Most of it was and is sheer pretext and showmanship that is steeped in four centuries of black preaching tradition in American Christendom. It boils down to little more than a form of self-aggrandizement that brings recognition to a man's preaching ability and acceptance in social and religious circles like nothing else can. Despite that, this church theater does lift the name of Christ. It helped black worshippers in the past transcend the horrors of America's social and economic apartheid. In the long run, these matters are certainly a big dose of what actually counts.

Again, now, as in the day of Christ, the devout held closely to their traditions and customs. They only saw right as they saw right, they saw sin as they saw sin, and wrong as they saw wrong; and, a human being was valuable only as they deemed them to be. This was the way their operative myopia worked in the case of the woman captured in adultery. Such shortsightedness diluted her humanity, and no amount of her sheer human need could have rescued her from their violence.

Christ rescued her. The religious of the day were obliged to see her only as her sin. The Lord saw her humanity and much beyond, not only her sin. When He stooped and wrote on the ground, there is the very real possibility that he wrote the names of the men standing there who were also guilty of adultery. Some of them stood and accused the woman to her face, right in His presence; while all the time, they knew they too, maybe not on that day, but certainly, they were as guilty as she of a divided heart.

For generations, pundits, intellectuals and scholars who observe the white black church divide equate its phenomenon with the same disturbing social hatreds and injustices that bred historical racism across every avenue of

American life. Most see and offer no path for reclamation of an attainable civility. What the intellectual conversations do, somehow, is to lend legitimacy to the structure and existence of behaviors that can never be supported within the strict context of the Judeo-Christian canon. Such arguments, perhaps, though not proved, may add life to the intransigent and unreasonable life span of sanctioned division in the Church as well as other serious and negative consequences of prejudice and bigotry. For instance, when respected historian E. Franklin Frazier says, ". . . It is no exaggeration to say that the 'invisible institution' of the Negro church took root among the enslaved blacks,[7] he is absolutely correct. However, the question then becomes: Where does the black church go in remapping its history—in reassigning itself a new role in the lives of a more progressive constituency? How does the black church move away from the identity of 'safe-haven' for those endangered by a hostile society before the Civil Rights gains of the 1950's and 1960's to that of a powerful broker of proactive strategies to inculcate true racial harmony?

According to the work of Lawrence Levine, Black *Culture and Black Consciousness*, ". . . Their cultural creations—their songs, music, dances, stories, art—transcend(s) any secular-sacred dichotomy. In fact, they were considered relevant for the whole of life; work, play and worship."[8] In contrast, over time, traditional white Christianity has become more compartmentalized. It separates from various segments of the lives of its members that which is sacred and that which is secular. Yet, many white Christians would be hard put, would even feel put upon if called racist. Case in point: On the Sunday that I met with my students who had gone on their interracial church visitations, just about forty miles from where we worshipped together, The Aryan Nation, the Skin Heads, and the Christian Identity Movement, met in a community reiterating their standard call for the separate existence of the races. I used a newspaper article to bring the event to a chat session with my students. The article was entitled: "Church to fight Aryans with love." In the article, a white pastor who organized an interdenominational, interracial prayer rally in response to gathering of the white supremacist was featured. In response, churches of every affiliation, white and black, gathered in front of the court house in Cincinnati to ward off the seriousness of the threat posed by these groups. The pastor said, "We believe that God will heal our land. The divisions in our city go beyond race . . . We do not want a confrontation with the Aryans. We don't want hate. We want unity in our city. We believe love will overcome hate."

Cincinnati is a city in a perpetual racial cauldron. For decades, little enthusiasm had surfaced by the churches to come together in support of "citywide unity." Even at the rally, the churches could be clearly identified as "black" and as "white." The irony is, and my senses reeled with the paradox, that before the Aryan march, except for the threat of violence, the churches were already practicing, every Lord's Day, the very separation of which the white supremacist insisted should be practiced. I am convinced that the life of change Christ wants for all believers is one that doesn't settle for tenuous peace or situational justice.

Someone must take the lead to see that the Church reflects the holiness, the life and character of God. With this in mind, I believe that for any substantive changes to occur in the fabric of white black worship healing, blacks may just have to take the forefront again as they did to bring down the wall of racial dichotomies in general society when these injustices could no longer be tolerated or found to be acceptable. Salvation, obedience to the commandments of God, and true religion transcends culture and tradition. When Christ said, 'be one as We are One,' He left no room or justification for hypocrisy.

Nevertheless, as scriptural history shows, when Jesus arose from His task of 'dirt writing,' so many centuries ago, not one accuser of the woman caught in adultery was left with him. No one bothered to remain to hear his message of change except the poor woman accused. Before Jesus left the tainted spot, He freed her from the killing bondage of religion and exonerated her life to move on with God.

Clearly, neither has God called Christians to a life of neutrality. The refusal of the devout to accept and embrace the deep flowing love of Christ, which brings change, made the Scribes and Pharisees dead men walking. This same ancient stagnation presently infuses the contemporary Church, both black and white, with pious dwarfism. Although one of the characteristics of church life in America has to do with the intractability of its practices, every person who names the name of Christ will have to decide as Joshua did: "Now if you are unwilling to serve the Lord, choose this day whom you will serve . . ." (Joshua 24:15).[9]

The change Christ sanctions requires an individual's willingness to initiate transformation from the inside first. Change that occurs from the inside has the power to inspire deep shifts in one's personal theology and culture that is promoted around it. After all, true worship of God invites God's presence into the midst. It is that which changes the hearts and the minds of men and women to truly follow Him—genuine worship is free of trappings and accompanying practices that limit the presence of God.

In the wilderness, God instructed Moses to build the Tabernacle. He gave specific instructions for building the tabernacle. To facilitate the effort, God asked for the best and purest forms of sacrifices and offerings in order to erect the holy structure: "And have them make me a sanctuary; so I may dwell among them. In accordance with all that I show you concerning the pattern of the tabernacle and its furniture, so you shall make it" (Exodus 24: 8, 9).[10]

Moreover, through the advent of Jesus and his work of reconciliation of humanity with God, amazingly, the very borders of these holy boundaries were altered and enlarged by a spiritual fiat of God. They were expanded to include anyone, and to free anyone who wanted to worship Him. Furthermore, Jesus made it absolutely clear that true worship would no longer be limited to a building. It emanates from the deepest recesses of a person's being. True worship taps our well spring of spiritual life. It infuses change within us that insists upon personal humility and the willingness of professed followers of Christ, to let go of traditions, behaviors, that likely have defined, for a lifetime—for even generations, who we think we are; often, despite the fact the image of Christ is yet to be realized in us, the "so called" professed followers.

In John 4: 23, 24, it is shown that true worship may take place anywhere: "But the hour is coming, and is now here, when the true worshipers shall worship the Father in spirit and truth, for the Father seeks such as these to worship him. God is a Spirit, and those who worship him must worship in spirit and truth."[11] Will we, today, allow God to instruct us how to build a tabernacle of worship in our wildernesses, so there, He can dwell?

NOTES

1. Eugene Genovese, *Roll Jordon Roll: The World the Slaves Made* (Pantheon Books, NY: 1974), 210.

2. Michael D. Coogan, Ed. *The New Oxford Annotated Bible: New Revised Standard Version with the Apocrypha* (Oxford University Press, New York, 2001), 162 [New Testament].

3. New Revised Standard Version with the Apocrypha, 162.

4. Gospel Pearls Song Book, first edition (Sunday School Publishing Board, National Baptist Convention, U.S.A. Nashville, Tennessee, 1921), 112.

5. Jonathan Alter, "America's 'Own Holocaust': A Historian finds the vestiges of slavery alive," Newsweek Interview, (December 8, 1997), 61.

6. Franklin M. Segler, *Christian Worship: It's Theology and Practice* (Broadman Press, Nashville, Tennessee, 1967), 52.

7. E. Franklin Frazier, *The Negro Church in America* (Schocken Books, New York, 1964), 23

8. Lawrence Levine, Black Culture and Black Consciousness (Oxford University, NY: 1977), 34.

9. New Revised Standard Version with the Apocrypha, 351 [Hebrew Bible].

10. New Revised Standard Version with the Apocrypha, 119 [Hebrew Bible].

11. New Revised Standard Version with the Apocryphal, 154 [New Testament].

Chapter Eight

The 21st Century Church:
A Covenant Community

I am aware of and appreciate the immense strides that have been made by worship communities, both black and white to include all who come together with them. I look forward to the day when these congregations, along with more traditional ones, will rise to the forefront as the 21st Century Church: a manifestation of unfolding Covenant communities; while these bands of believers blossom under the will of God with life and healing balms of reconciliation. I look forward to the day also when these kinds of worshipful gathering places are the rule and not the exception to what worship communities look like in America's future.

I know, there are Christians in the Church who do not care who worships among them. Both black and white parishioners are doing all they know to live out the mandates of God in love and union as demonstrated by Christ. Because He has said, "Love one another," these use love as pure as they know and understand it as the basis and foundation of transcending the specific issues of separation based on race and ethnicity when they gather together in the name of Jesus. For them, the age old observance of separation in fellowship based on the color of ones skin, on family traditions and cultural practices, does no more than overshadow the intent and purpose of the presence of the Holy Spirit in the midst of them, God's people.

It must be remembered, it was pride that inspired whites, based on a lie, (that they are superior to blacks) to enslave blacks. The principle underpinning of slavery was pride—an act of lifting oneself above the knowledge and will of God. And in response, it was a sense of fear, entrapment and sorrow that held blacks in physical, spiritual and psychological bondage for three centuries. None of the motives of this tragedy helped the cause of it on either side. Whites dehumanized blacks as a way to justify their behavior toward them. In each generation leading up to the actual act of Emancipation, blacks found ways to reclaim their humanity. Whether it was in a song, in a spiritual song, or in a hymn; to subvert their suffering, they did what came naturally to pursue freedom, and to overcome all of the deprivations that were tenets of the unusual practices of American slavery and the subsequent apparatuses of apartheid. Indeed, the enormous scope of the system of slavery and the separation it bred led to a two-tiered society in America that finally collapsed and proved that such unrighteousness cannot prevail in the presence of God. To enter Covenant with God means that Christians of every ilk and stripe must abandon their own wills to the express will of God. It stands to reason then, that in a changing and culturally diverse society of worshippers, Church leaders necessarily have to confront important institutional issues related to conforming in order to respond openly and lovingly to the needs of all of God's children in an atmosphere of genuine inclusion.

Lyle Schaller, one of the leading writers on church growth and congregational life, said, in his work: The very Large Church: New Rules for Leaders raises essential questions relevant to current and future discussions that result from a changing religious culture. Some of the questions he asks are:

> Do you believe that the best road to racial integration of the churches will be to place the primary emphasis on encouraging American-born blacks to join predominately Anglo congregations? Or should the primary emphasis on encouraging white churchgoers to join predominately African American Churches? Or to organize multiethnic missions?[1]

Schaller's questions are reflective and pose an honest and forthright approach to assessing the racial landscape in America. These questions can become part of the crucial contemplations and mediations that Christians are obliged to consider in regards to sincere racial reconciliation among black and white churches. Needless to say, that in order to move forward, everyone who is encumbered with the mental and emotional baggage of a society, which is bereft of any sound biblical ideology on race relations, but is, in fact, seared with stereotypes and misrepresentations of one another; ways must be sought that aim us toward freeing the Church of Christ from spiritual, secular and traditional bondage. Even if the American Church does not somehow triumph and eventually free itself from these besetting weights, the world watches and will always do so. Unfortunately, what it sees presently and will continue to see in the future if it does not change, are the mixed messages of our divided faith and uncertain spiritual consciousness.

A former Lutheran pastor, author and missionary to West Africa; nearly fifty years ago, Walter Trobisch, echoed this sentiment when he shared a conversation he had while in Africa,

> As I was riding on an African train last year, one of my fellow travelers asked me: "Are those people in America who still cling to racial segregation and discrimination Christians?' He knew the answer, of course. He knew that some of them are Christians. His conclusion was clear: If that is true, then Christianity has no message for us. We must wake up to the fact that there are no longer any isolated actions possible in this world of ours, so that in a much greater measure than before every individual becomes a strategic figure on one of two battlefields—either God's or the devil's. If we [American Christians] want to be part of world missions today, and if we start to think strategically, we have to awaken people in America to the fact that our failure to settle the race problems in this country may result in the loss of the African continent for Christ.[2]

One half century later, from the time of Trobisch's insights, finds American Christians no farther along the path of surrender and reconciliation. Though his conversation took place during the beginnings of the upheavals of the Civil Rights Movement, people in Africa were fully aware of the plight that their brothers and sisters in the Diaspora suffered in America. With racial strife and hatred as a backdrop and as a surly undertow to life in America, what a paradox to sincerity the message of the love of Christ had to have suffered in Africa. America's racial duality no doubt presented for missionaries on the field, in Africa in particular, who attempted to spread the Gospel message a challenge almost undefeatable. And ultimately, in America, what Christian life boiled down to then in Africa is still a slow boil today around the world. The hypocrisy that exists between Christian love and racial separation is a dilemma at home and abroad that cannot avoid casting aspersions on the credible message of truth that is the Gospel of our Lord and Savior Jesus Christ.

Consider the thoughts of Everett Harrison: the original concept of Covenant (Berit) as expressed during the Old Testament period signified ". . . a relationship between two parties wherein each bound himself to perform a certain service for the other."[3] Genuine spiritually begins with a strong and enduring bond between God and His people. The fullest expression of this bond is the manifestation of unconditional love by His people back to Him and to one another as well as to others not yet in the fold of His Kingdom. I am certain that all people are created in God's image and as such must be accorded the dignity and value inherent in their God given humanity. Since God is no respecter of persons, Christians must not be inordinately selective either. Christians, as servants, have to accept and respect this: that God had the freedom of His own prerogative to create human beings in His image as He so chose to do. Not with merit and accuracy can anyone deem unclean what God has made clean except, that is, to "exalt themselves above the knowledge of God." Any time that this pride-filled path is chosen, adversity ensues. As Gustavo Guiterrez writes, "Sin is in effect a refusal to love others and consequently, a refusal to love the Lord. According to the Bible, sin, or the breaking off of friendship with God and others, is the ultimate cause of want, injustice, and oppression in which human beings live."[4] Likewise, Steven L. McKenzie writes, ". . . segregation is not just undesirable, but is an affront to God and defeats the very purpose for which Christ came to earth."[5]

Just like the self-importance of racial supremacy is the underpinning of all that brings separation between any people in any complex social or religious arrangements, love must be the major principle and controlling attribute of a Christ-centered community of Covenant. That is to say, if we Christians love our neighbor as ourselves, we will seek only what is the most edifying and uplifting for one another. In the event that racism is not the reason why so many white churches still remain almost lily white, the world will never know that, given the history—the traditions and culture of it—if that church, is looked upon, in its current posture, as an example. If blacks were truly forgiving of those who have brought offense against them, it is not so apparent by the lack of outreach to their white counterparts in Christ since the church remains and functions almost in the same way it did a half century ago. The 'I Shall Not Be Moved' status quo of American churches eclipses any opportunity for the Church to emerge, as members of the body of Christ must, to pursue the real mission of Christian spirituality: to help people grow to their fullest potential. Of course, the real mission remains dormant as long as everyone chooses to stay dug into their own trenches and refuse to move one iota.

Naturally, the Church divided by race and racism will never grow to its fullest potential. It cannot. The word of God says, "a house divided against itself cannot stand" (Matthew 12:25). Everything done in the name of Christ, must be united around the purposes of Christ, unity being the first, if it is to prosper. It is revealed Covenant, and throughout the Old Testament, God gave His chosen people their unique identity, solidarity and ultimately their sense of community. Much earlier in this text, I questioned the place of Jewish expressionism in their traditions of worship—whether or not their particular experiences have inculcated a worship style representative of an outgrowth of their specific circumstances. My answer to this inquiry has to be an overwhelming, "Yes!" From ancient times, Jews have cultivated a unique worship experience and have preserved their history that reminds them from whence they came and of God who brought them. Their religious experience is intertwined tightly in their life of ancient slavery in Egypt and genocide in Europe.

All of their experiences are tied to their history of near mythical triumph over human struggle and hardship. Yet, their tradition, too, cannot remain so very cloistered that it is not a vital part of the broad community of the faithful who aspire to a coalition of unity and reconciliation between those who say they know, deify and pray to the Holy God. According to Janet K. O'Dea, Thomas F. O'Dea and Charles J. Adams, who wrote, *Judaism, Christianity and Islam*, "They accepted the covenant as a gift of the Lord which would establish a permanent relationship between Him and them . . . The loose tribes were transformed into people united by shared loyalty to Yahweh, and ordered in political and social realms by his religious code."[6] While this assessment is correct; within this special and permanent relationship, with God, and with one another comes the responsibility to join all who worship the God of Israel to legitimately seek and broker unity in His name.

The huge fault line that divides American religions seem to be too much of an obstacle to overcome in this lifetime; nevertheless, it is not. It requires a transformation of everyone's attitudes, and perseverance to overcome obstructions to the bidding and purposes of God. For many, the teachings, declarations and traditions of their worship communities appear bold and resolute in their rightness. And based on this worldview of insularity, the majority of American worshipers have no desire or intention to change. As a matter of fact, at times, the word of God may seem a docile footnote in comparison to their church doctrines and customs. The word of God seems unable in its ability to persuade and change minds and hearts in favor of obedience to God. It does one well, however, to keep in mind that the ways and thoughts of man are temporal. Someday, in God's time and judgment, all of the towers constructed in the name of religion will be moved off earth's mortal strain. On the other hand, there is nothing quite as dramatic and enduring as the word of God. There is nothing at all about the word of God that we may expect to be moved or changed, to fade away in order to accommodate the fleeting traditions and customs of the current church structures.

Ideally, as we enter the 21st century, according to Robert Webber, it is time for a paradigm shift. "Paradigm thinking provides us with an intelligent way to deal with times of transition."[7] This paradigm shift appeals to a new and dynamic approach to understanding the role of a postmodern Church in a postmodern society that will allow itself to become, at last, an expression of the life of Christ. After all, Christ said, "For I have come down from heaven, not to do my own will, but the will of Him who sent me . . ." (John 6:38). Should not the modern church find its purpose in this same challenging paradigm as Jesus did? He, in seeking not to do His own will, but the will of His Father, in a horrifying, but magnificent and conquering gesture, laid down his life to reconcile the world to God.

Traditionally, Christians have viewed the institutions of the black and white church as two separate entities, which they most certainly are in this country. But no aspect of this worldview has ever incorporated the idea of the Church, of which these two entities are a part, in a faithful and unitary role, existing solely as one organism to build the kingdom of God—and nothing more. ". . . Your kingdom come, Your will be done on earth as it is in heaven. . ." (Matthew 6:10).[8] Surely, as compliant witnesses to the kingdom of God, it is crucial that Christians use the Gospel message for evangelization and to begin to, more vigorously than ever work toward dismantling divisive schisms within the family of God. As Christians, our hope of a heavenly home is certainly not to be understood as "two homes, one white and the other black." Let us all read again the words of our Lord. Allow them to sink deep into our hearts. ". . . Your will be done on earth as in heaven." Here on earth, I submit, is a good place to begin practicing what we surely await, with expectant souls, to experience in heaven.

NOTES

1. Lyle E. Schaller, *The Very Large Church: New Rules for Leaders* (Abingdon Press, Nashville, Tennessee, 2000), 237.

2. Walter Trobisch, "God's World Strategy" originally published under the title "This Was Not Done on a Corner" in (Evangelize Magazine, October 1957), 741.

3. Everett F. Harrison, Geoffrey W. Bromiley, and Carl F. Henry, ed. *Wycliffe Dictionary of Theology* (Hendrickson Publishers, Baker Books Division, Grand Rapids, Michigan, 1999), 142.

4. Gustavo Guiterrez, *The Truth Should Make You Free* (Orbis Books, Maryknoll, New York, 1990), 15.

5. Steven L. *McKenzie, All God's Children: A Biblical Critique of Racism* (Westminster John Knox Press, Louisville, Kentucky, 1997), 114.

6. Janet K. O'Dea, Thomas F. O'Dea and Charles J. Adams, ed. Judaism, *Christianity and Islam* (Harper & Row Publishers, New York, 1972), 5.

7. Robert Webber, *Ancient-Future Faith: Rethinking Evangelism for a Postmodern World* (Baker Books, Grand Rapids, Michigan, 1999), 17.

8. Michael D. Coogan, ed., *The New English Bible with the Apocrypha* (Oxford University Press, Cambridge University Press, 1970), [16, New Testament]

Chapter Nine

Changed Attitudes: Transformed Church

In order for the Church to transform its image and to reestablish its purpose and mission in America and around the world, and to become the powerful significant entity of its potential, attitudes will have to change. Despite the fact that semantic vagueness has surrounded the term "Church" since its inception, the word has always been used to distinguish religious people from non-religious people. Further, its meaning connotes the institution around which the teachings of Christ coalesce. The term "Church" has been used denominationally to draw lines in the sand between doctrines and worship preferences. Groups have branded themselves with such nomenclatures as Presbyterian, Methodist, Catholic, and Baptist. The expression, "Church" has also been used to describe a building or physical meeting place of adherents to a particular teaching.

However, what Christians have designated as the "Church," Jesus saw Himself as the embodiment of that, without the benefit of a building or an institution while He lived among people. After all, the works He left yet to be done on the earth, down through the ages, specifically involves people and not institutions. Jesus made no distinction between different peoples. His walk through Samaria and that momentous encounter with the woman at the well tore down a longstanding wall of division by experience and example for His admirers and followers. He charged His disciples to do what he did; that is, to touch the lives of hurting needy people.

Jesus never formally organized or established any denominational or ethnic house of worship. They later, His disciples, became the "Church" after His departure. It is not clear in the scriptures that He gave instructions for, or ever intended institutions to form. Still, Christ did not abandon His followers. Ernest Payne, when confronted with the question "What does the Church give?"

writes that "The Church gives us the life of the incarnate Christ."[1] However, while incarnate, Jesus was pleased to mentor that loose band of Jewish adherents whom He gave an opportunity to see into His heart. And what they saw was the friend, advocate, protector and provider for those persons who were sick, destitute, and who in many ways were socially, economically and spiritually dispossessed. They were the least in society; most often powerless to meet their own daily needs. In effect, what they witnessed was the heart of a servant who lived to interact with God's most precious creation. They saw into the heart of the One who came to do only the will of His Father.

For me, it does not require a grand leap of faith or imagination to assume that He wanted His disciples to be and do the same as He had done. To continue to minister to the neediest was the parting benediction of the Lord to His followers. "All power in heaven and in earth . . . Go ye therefore and teach . . . teaching them to observe all things whatsoever I have commanded you: and lo, I am with you always, even unto the end of the world" (Matthew 28: 18-20) was a request and an encouragement that gave credence to this idea of continued ministry to deprived and disadvantaged people in whatever state or form His devotees exists. In these words rests a mandate. It is difficult to construe it to mean anything other than that as long as the earth remains, He expects his supporters to continue the perennial work of God—of drawing men [women] to Him—of restoring a spiritual innocence to the relationship between God and Mankind, hence with one another; in other words, to do—the work of healing and reconciliation.

After His ascension, Jesus' disciples fanned out across the Middle East, Africa, Asia Minor, Greece, Rome and Italy to spread the Gospel. In spite of their tenuous understanding of their Leader and his works, they were ever so fervent in their missionary efforts. They grew as they went. It is said that they were so effective: 'they turned the world upside down.'

Disparate ideologies, nevertheless, grew around the departure of their various locations and evangelistic aims. In the first quarter century, after Jesus' departure, starting with those early groups, efforts to try and encompass the magnitude of the Lord fueled a metamorphosis of personal doctrines and ways of worship. Men have always sought to understand their fleeting places in this boundless universe. They try and understand their relationship with the invisible God. To this day, monumental questions persist about Jesus, (who was He really?) rather than focus on the prescience of his labors. Yet from time to time, new sects and doctrines still emerge that proffer new revelations about Jesus and his uniqueness—The Man, His works; He is still a flash point for personal interpretations of God, and what God's real deeds on the earth might now be. Most man-centered doctrines and traditions circumvent the simplicity of Jesus' life and His motivational directives.

During the early centuries, particularly those closest to Christ's time on earth, rampant personal interpretations began to spawn sects and movements that captured narrow inward foci, intellectual foci, even a self-absorbed nihilistic focus, instead of the motivational focus in which is maintained the power as ascribed by God to carry forth with the greater works ministry He told them they would inherit. Yet, it is not unnatural that such a persona as mysterious and as Holy as Jesus should inspire great thirst and hunger in people to know God, to long for and to seek Him. Nonetheless, because the truths of the living God are parallel, they ideally ought to have led seekers together, from the beginning, in their search for certainty and meaning, back to the parting words of Jesus' grace with only one agenda to pursue. Instead, what proliferates even to this day are distinct bands of believers, separate and apart, that characterizes a disjointed movement of Christianity called the Church that on the world stage grows to be ever more so.

Identity shifts that have moved the Church away from the life and central purpose of Jesus have been a mainstay of its history. In the roiling life of the late twentieth century Church, for instance, men and women built personal empires whereby they have amassed huge individual fortunes and international fame based on the name, life and work of the Lord. They captured the attention of vulnerable people thirsty to know God with so-called new revelations from Him predicated on a theology of greed. These leaders convinced untold millions of people of their own importance in the presence of Almighty God that made claims of their uniqueness and intermediary status with Him. These took from people rather than give to them. Many Christians began to and still follow these men and women in the guise of following God. The corrupt practice of charging people for absolution of their sins is what eventually led to Martin Luther's Reformation. This cynical practice by segments of the modern church of separating adherents from their money for blessings from God is nothing less than an equivalent practice.

Also, during the late twentieth century the church saw the rise of fundamentalist groups like The Moral Majority, the Christian Coalition, and many others sprang to the forefront of Christian life and started moves of ultra exclusivity. Humphreys and Wise have well articulated in their book, *Fundamentalism* saying, "Fundamentalist are like an army that sets up outposts to defend a city and then begins to think the outposts are themselves the city."[2] Their momentum actually espoused a disdain for the general populous and for those who do not embrace their worldview—mostly, the world yet to be reconciled to God. A "them and us" doctrine bred creeds which do not indicate God's love for the people He wants drawn to Him. Over time, these organizations sought political power and currently have gained a strong voice in the halls of American politics.

Jesus, on the other hand, apparently saw politics differently. "In a sense, Jesus was the ultimate activist in that he dedicated his entire being to struggling to bring the world in line with the vision of love, liberation, and justice given to him by God.[3] It was an arena He entered only to challenge it and to buffet it. He shook and troubled those crooked politicians of his day. Arguably, in no era was politics more violent or mean spirited than in the time that Jesus lived. But he did not become the bedfellow of corrupt politicians to accomplish his spiritual goals. He became an out-and out thorn in the side of the Priests and ancient political machinery of Rome that dominated Israel. He loved the people oppressed by it, and sought to give them a transcendent outlook by which they could overcome its hard tasks. He preached in the synagogues, albeit a message so astounding, the institutional clergymen of his era were alarmed to their cores. And in the last hours of His life, with all power in heaven and in earth in His hands and at His disposal, He did not even bother to dignify the inquiries of immoral politicians and dishonest churchmen with answers.

Today, Christians and their leaders must thirst and hunger for God's pure righteousness. They must shun everything except the will of God. In the present day, church leaders proudly showcase themselves with politicians and strike hands with them to achieve aims so limited that the voice of Jesus' final words, "All power is given unto me in heaven and in earth" (Matthew 28:18) is no longer immediate enough for them. Those words do not strongly resonate, if at all, in American churches; indeed, not in those so willing and ready to align themselves with the sordid impotence of corrupt politics. Spiritual drift characterizes the Church in our day. Racial politics, as the powerful generational lynchpin it has been, is a major contributor to this regrettable state of affairs. If the Church is to move in the power and potency of Christ, then Christ has to be its main constituent, and the attitude that it can be empowered by anything or anyone other than He has got to change.

The Church will realize a revolution of transformation when ethnicity, race, gender, and class are relegated to a status much lower than its current elevation. The desire to please and do God's will must be elevated to a top position in the hearts and minds of all Christians regardless of race, traditions or customs. In spite of the fundamental orientation of the Church to serve the pressing needs of its various groups, a theological repositioning, which moves it to a Christ centered entity will energize it with new life in Christ. Colossians 3:17-18, says, "And he is before all things and by him all things consist. And he is the head of the body, the church: who is the beginning, the firstborn from the dead; that in all things he might have the preeminence." When Christ's followers organized, He was not organized out of the picture. That was not their intention. According to Robert Webber, "Our calling is not to reinvent the Christian faith, but, in keeping with the past, to carry forward what the church has affirmed from the beginning."[4]

Finally, in Christ is salvation and adoption into the family of God, "Where there is neither Jew nor Greek, bond nor free, but all are one in Him" (Colossians 3:11). As a Covenant Community of transformed believers, a return of commitment to the biblical principal of unity is vital for persons within the kingdom of God. One cannot know what the church gives apart from knowing, as Payne suggests, "the inside knowledge of one who really shares in the intimate life of a community."[5] Thus, the Church, across racial boundaries, has to function as the pathway of intimate relational fellowship (Koinonia) between all Christians. Unless, however, Christians are willing to encounter one another across racial boundaries, the gathered assembly of all of God's people will never be realized. The Church is the spiritual family of God and as such, it is essential that it not be defined or limited by color or ethnicity.

NOTES

1. Ernest A. Payne, *Fellowship of Believers Baptist: Baptist Thought and Practice* (The Kingsgate Press, Southampton Row, London, 1944), 5

2. Fisher Humphreys and Philip Wise, *Fundamentalism* (Smyth & Helwys Publishing, Macon, Georgia, 2004), 95.

3. Obey M. Hendricks, Jr., *The Politics of Jesus: Rediscovering the True Revolutionary Nature of Jesus' Teaching and How They Have Been Corrupted* (Doubleday Publishing, New York, 2006), 93.

4. Robert Webber, *Ancient-Future Faith: Rethinking For a Postmodern World* (Baker Books, Grand Rapids, Michigan, 1999), 17.

5. ———. Payne, 5.

Chapter Ten

A Final Word on the Theology of Integration

Jesus' certitude of inclusion brought those at the farthest rims of society into places of empowerment. A man blind from birth received his sight; a man who had sat by the pool of Bethesda for nearly forty years waiting for help was given strength to get himself into the pool; a woman who had been oppressed for twelve years with bloodletting was at last made well. After centuries of being a repository of suffering and protectionism; but most of all, a spiritual sanctuary, under the universal leadership of Dr. Martin Luther King, Jr. and the Southern Leadership Conference, the black church took an unprecedented stand of moral and civil leadership. Spiritually, Dr. King's theology of integration mirrored that of Jesus' demonstrations of conviction to include all when setting captives free. Not only were blacks liberated from lives of moral and civic decay, but integration and fairness set everyone in America free to live better lives of genuine respect for humanity.

Not all, including many in the Church, agreed with the trajectory of Dr. King's leadership and philosophy; nevertheless, racism was a heavy burden for the country to continue to bare. The time was right and the system had to be changed. In the grips of racial duplicity, America was not meeting its obligations to all it citizens and by default was not living up to its strength, power and significance as a nation nor as a world leader. The situation that existed with the Church historically in America continues to be true today, and for all appearances, is true for the foreseeable path of the 21st century Church. Nonetheless, as the representative of the nature and will of God, the Church is obliged to become intolerant of that which is not representative of the character of Him. Until and unless the church mirrors the motivational purposes of Jesus on behalf of God, its spiritual significance and power is limited.

Make no mistake, the light of the Church is currently a beacon to those who lack hope, but seek hope for better lives. It is a lifeline to uncountable families and individuals in America and is a conduit of salvation and deliverance to millions of people around the world. In as much as the Church fills a place in American society and the world that no other institution can fill, it is essential in its role to the lives so many people live. Yet, God still calls to the Church—that it should rise, without duplicity, to its ultimate spiritual power and become the strong force in the earth that Christ intended his followers to display.

With sureness, in the 1950's and 1960's, the black church became the moral and civic conscious of America in an era when the country needed to be awakened to the gravity of its moral and civic unrighteousness. At the same time, while rising to this important role of unprecedented leadership, the black church thrust itself out of the role of the longsuffering servant into the proactive stance of one that challenged effete forces of social oppression. Not since the Civil War had America, as a country, been forced to face its racial indiscretion at the level of its deep and embittered roots. The Civil Rights Movement with its demands required the country to acknowledge that a dual and unequal society was morally wrong and for the Church to acknowledge that such conditions were spiritually unacceptable. Once and for all, profound and mutli-layered changes had to be mandated because nothing less would suffice. Socially, as evidenced by subsequent changes, the country made legal bounds that moved it toward a more inclusive society. The changes have by and large been for the betterment of all in the country.

In the midst of the upheaval of the Civil Rights Movement, the white church was unplaced, unmoved and unseated from its stance of separateness, and thus has continued pretty much as it always has. The black church, I argue, stopped far too short of its next step to grapple with a spiritual phase of outreach and the push for even greater change in the nation. According to Robert Webber, "The kind of Christianity that attracts the new generation of Christians and will speak effectively to a postmodern world is one that emphasizes primary truths and authentic embodiment . . . more attracted to an inclusive view of the faith than an exclusive view, more concerned with unity than diversity, more open to dynamic, growing faith than to a static fixed system. . ."[1]

Webber's proposal calls for proactive grassroots leadership, much like that of the Civil Rights Movement, which crosses racial and denominational boundaries. My work, however, neither expects nor recommends nor thinks it possible or feasible to eradicate the black church or the white church. I do not advocate posing unwanted advances of one group over the will of another.

What I do propose is that the basis of authentic Christianity ought to reflect a moral and biblical philosophy of equality. Ideally, the beginnings of a real covenant community will start with the affirmation of the authority of the scriptures. For this to occur, both institutions, the black church and the white church, have to eradicate the distinctions of ethnicity and race from their gatherings of believers. Such a paradigmatic shift inevitably invites the life and Spirit of God to do the transforming work necessary to bridge the lives of all Christians.

Forgiveness, the genuine spirit of it, begins with the power of consent. Optimally, exemplary righteousness must duly challenge the Church in America from now until Christ returns. It has an obligation to the Great Commission to move beyond the static nature of tradition and the cultural limits that have stifled its progress toward maturity and inclusiveness. Such a brave confrontation of an issue so personal and close to the hearts of so many will involve every person who claims the name of Jesus Christ and His principals as a guiding force in their lives to surrender to Him anew. I know, and everyone who has lived life steeped in tradition knows that nothing is as hard to accomplish as change; that no step is as hard to take as the first step. On the other hand, the only way to full participation by Christians in the glorious mysteries of the life of Christ can only be inspired by an irrepressible desire of the faithful to truly follow Him.

Peace, social justice, human dignity, enduring hardships were all attributes that marked the life and character of Christ. These strengths are they which overrode the adversities He suffered in defense of man. In the end, he gave his life for the issues that were central to His ministry to the entire planet. Peace and social justice, concern for the poor and elevation of the disenfranchised were ideals that motivated the works and contributions of Dr. Martin Luther King, Jr. His imagination was fired by his desire to see equalitarianism other than a facile aspect of American life. Following in the footsteps of his Savior, Dr. King laid down his life for spiritual righteousness while he lived and eventually made the ultimate sacrifice for what he believed: in essence, "To whom much is given, much is required"(Luke 12:48).

The same exacting cost for establishing the perimeters of the ministry of Christ is required of the Church. Only it has the sole authority to promote the hegemony of God's power in the nation and around the world. Only it can drive a stake in the heart of separation and racial exclusivity; and though the move to do so has to start with each parishioner, realistically, it has to start somewhere with someone. Perhaps, the primary overtures for the consent of forgiveness may well have to start with black worshippers in America. As the most offended group in American society, it may be they who have to embrace the grace to "bring their gifts to the altar . . . [and] first be reconciled to his brother, and then come and offer [their gifts to God].

NOTE

1. Robert E. Webber, *Ancient-Future Faith: Rethinking Evangelicalism for a Postmodern World* (baker Books, Grand Rapids, Michigan, 199), 27.

Group Discussion Questions

The following questions and scripture references are intended to facilitate inter-ethnic cultural communication, as well as foster further discussion on the chapter themes of the book.

CHAPTER ONE. THE EMERGENCE OF THE
CHURCH AND ITS PLACE IN AMERICAN SOCIETY

- Historically what role has tradition and familial habits played in shaping black and white churchgoers perspectives on race? On what do you base your response?
Read: Matthew 15:1-3; Galatians 1:10-15; Colossians 2:8
- Do you see anything wrong with the separation of Christian worshipers based upon race and ethnicity? On what do base your response?
Read: St. John 4:20-24; Acts 17:25-28

CHAPTER TWO. THE ROLE OF THE
BLACK CHURCH IN A FRAGMENTED SOCIETY

- Do you see any contradictions, in either black or white church traditions, or familial habits as it relates to Christian theology and biblical mandates?
Read: I Corinthians 3:1-10; St. John 17:21-23; Galatians 3:26-29
- The church remains a significant institution in American culture and life. With that reality, can you name at least three positive and or practical steps white and black churchgoers have taken in bridging the racial divide?

CHAPTER THREE. THE AMERICAN FAMILY, CHURCH TRADITION AND THEOLOGY

- What is your understanding of the importance of tradition in the formation of Christian Theology and can, or should we assess spiritual formation in the context of racial unity?
  Read: II Thessalonians 2:3-17; I Peter1:18-22; Philippians 2:8-10
- Do you believe that the integration of Christian worshipers across racial lines would help to resolve much of the racial problems in America? On what do you base your response?
  Read: Romans 12:1-5; Matthew 5:13-16; Mark 9:50; Hebrews 12:14

CHAPTER FOUR. SACRED, SECULAR, OR MERELY SINFUL

- Is the sacred nature of worship different in the black Christian tradition than the white Christian tradition? If there are differences, how might these differences contribute to the perpetuation of the separation between black and white worshipers? On what do you base your response?
  Read: St. John 4:23-24; Ephesians 5:18-20 Psalm 95:1-7; 96:1-13;
- Do black and white churchgoers worship styles differ or are they similar to the extent, that these styles influence authentic worship? What is it about the style of worship at your church that appeals most to you?
  Read: Matthew 15:8, 9; Psalm 47:1; 149:1; 150

CHAPTER FIVE. THE HIGH COST OF RECONCILIATION

- Have you ever worshiped across racial lines where your race or ethnic group might be considered the minority? If you answered yes, how did the worship experience effect you?
  Read: Matthew 5:24; Ephesians 2:16-19; II Corinthians 5:18;
- Have you ever worshiped across racial lines where your race or ethnic group was considered in the minority? If so, has that experience positively or negatively shaped your perception of either white or black styles of worship? On what do you base your response?

CHAPTER SIX. THE FANCIFUL
INTERPLAY OF COLOR AND CULTURE

- What role has the media played historically in perpetuating stereotypes and preconceived notions involving black and white Christian worshipers? Give examples of books, movies and other media venues and discuss ways in which race is portrayed.
Read: Ephesians 5:4-7; Philippians 2:1-4
- What are your views regarding competition for leadership positions in the local church, and does that competition in anyway impact upon the separation of black and white Christian worshipers? On what do you base your response?
Read: I Corinthians 3:1, Galatians 5:26; I Corinthians 7:7; James 1:17

CHAPTER SEVEN. THE LAYERS OF
MEANING FOUND IN RELIGIOUS WORLDVIEWS

- Do you believe that there exist today, traditional African (religious) elements in black American worship, culture and life, elements which constitute a different sacred worldview? If so, what might those elements be?
- What do you believe is the logical and practical response to reconciliation between black and white Christian worshipers?
Read: I John 4:7-8; Ephesians 4:1-2; Hebrew 12:1-2

CHAPTER EIGHT. THE 21ST CENTURY CHURCH:
A COVENANT COMMUNITY

- Do you believe that integration of Christian worshipers across racial lines provides an effective witness to the Christian principle of unity and inclusion in the family of God?
Read: Acts 1:8; 10:9-16; Revelation 5:9
- The Bible refers to the church as the "body of Christ" and the "Kingdom of God". How might those descriptions support or oppose the aim of integrated worshiping communities across racial lines?
Read: I Corinthians 12:12-19; Ephesians 4:9-16; 5:28-30

CHAPTER NINE. CHANGED ATTITUDES: TRANSFORMED CHURCH

- Should the work of racial reconciliation be a significant priority for the Christian church in America?
Read: II Corinthians 5:19; Ephesians 2:16
- Do you believe a church should today be identified along ethnic or color lines, such as the "Black Church" or the "White Church"?
Read: Acts 2:47; 20:18; Ephesians 5:25; I Timothy 5:16

CHAPTER TEN. A FINAL WORD ON THE THEOLOGY OF INTEGRATION

- During the Civil Rights Movement, Dr. Martin Luther King, Jr., and others suggested that "eleven O' clock Sunday Morning" was the most segregated hour in America; in your opinion do those words still hold true today?
- Do we have any reason to be hopeful or optimistic concerning the Christian Church in respect to racial reconciliation in America?

Bibliography

Alter Jonathan, "America's 'Own Holocaust': A Historian finds the vestiges of slavery alive," *Newsweek*. (December 8, 1997), 61.

Baldwin, Lewis. *There is a Balm in Gilead: The Cultural Roots of Dr. Martin Luther King, Jr.* Minneapolis, MN: Fortress Press, 1991.

Barna, George. *The Second Coming of the Church.* Nashville, Word Publishing, 1998.

Byrd, Terriel R. *Non-African American Perception of the African American Religious Experience: How that Perception Impacts 11:00 Sunday Morning Being the Most Segregated Hour in American Life.* Ann Arbor, Michigan, UMI Dissertation Services, 1999.

Carol, Stream. "She has a dream, too" *Christianity Today* (June 16, 1997):36.

Cone, James H. For *My People: Black Theology the Black Church?* Mary Knoll, New York, Orbis Books, 1984.

Coogan Michael D., Ed. The New Oxford Annotated Bible: New Revised Standard Version with the Apocrypha. New York, Oxford University Press, 2001.

Davies, Alfred T., Ed. *The Pulpit Speaks on Race.* New York, Abingdon Press, 1965.

Drummond Lewis A. *The Evangelist.* Nashville, Tennessee, Word Publishing, 2001.

Durkheim, Emile. *The Elementary Forms of Religious Life.* New York, Macmillan Publishing, 1965.

Dyson, Michael E. *Race Rules: Navigating the Color Line.* New York, Random House, 1997.

Emerson, Michael O., and Christian Smith. *Divided by Faith: Evangelical Religion and the Problem of Race in America.* New York, Oxford University Press, 2000.

Evans, Tony. *Are Blacks Spiritually Inferior to Whites: Dispelling of an American Myth* Wenonah, NJ: Renaissance Productions, Inc. 1992.

Frazier, Franklin E. *The Negro Church in America.* New York, Schocken Books, 1964.

Fulop, Timothy E., and Albert J. Raboteau. *African-American Religion: Interpretive Essays in History and Culture.* New York & London, Routledge, 1979.

Garraty, John A. ed. *Historical Viewpoint: Notable Articles from American Heritage*, Third Edition, Volume One to 1877. New York, Harper & Row, 1979.

Gates, Henry Louis Jr., and Cornel West. *The Future of the Race.* New York, Vintage Books, 1996.

Gauss, James F. *We the People, Volume II: Birth of a Nation. Bloomington,* IN: Lightning Source, Inc., 2004.

Genovese, Eugene. *Roll Jordon Roll: The World the Slaves Made.* New York, Pantheon Books, 1974.

Gilreath, Edward, associate ed. "The Forgotten Founder". *Christianity Today,* (March 2002): 68.

Guiterrez, Gustavo. *The Truth Should Make You Free.* Maryknoll, New York, Orbis Books, 1990.

Harrison, Everett F., Geoffrey W. Bromiley, and Carl F. Henry, ed. *Wycliffe Dictionary of Theology.* Hendrickson Publishers, Grand Rapids, Michigan, 1999.

Hendricks, Obery M. Jr. *The Politics of Jesus: Rediscovering the True Revolutionary Nature of the Teachings of Jesus and How They Have Been Corrupted.* New York, Doubleday Publishing, 2006.

Hickman, Hoyt L. *A Primer for Church Worship.* Nashville, Tennessee, Abingdon Press, 1984.

Hudson, Winthrop S. *Religion in America: An historical account of the development of American religious life.* New York, Macmillian Publishing, 1987.

Humphreys, Fisher and Philip Wise. *Fundamentalism.* Macon, Georgia, Smyth & Helwys Publishing, 2004.

Kautz, Steven "Liberalism and the Idea of Toleration," American Journal of Political Science, Vol.37, No.2 (May, 1993):610-632.

Kehrberg, Kirk D. Park Ranger, Colonial NHP, "The First Legislative Assembly at Jamestown, Virginia," Colonial National Historical Park 1999, http://www.nps.gov/colo/jthanout/1stASSLY.html (July 25, 2006).

King, Martin Luther Jr., James M. Washington, ed. *Testament of Hope: The Essential Writings and Speeches of Martin Luther King, Jr.* San Francisco, Harper Collins, 1991.

King, Martin Luther Jr. *Where Do We Go From Here: Chaos or Community?* New York, Harper & Row Publishers, 1967.

Leffler, William J. II, and Paul H. Jones. *The Structure of Religion: Judaism and Christianity.* Lanham, Maryland, University Press of America, Inc.:2005.

Levine, Lawrence. *Black Culture and Black Consciousness.* New York, Oxford University Press, 1977.

Mays, Benjamin E., and Joseph W. Nicholson. *The Negro's Church.* New York: Institute of Religious Research, 1933.

McKenzie, Steven L. *All God's Children: Biblical Critique of Racism.* Louisville, Kentucky, Westminster John Knox Press, 1997.

Nelsen, Hart M., and Anne K Nelsen. *Black Church in the Sixties.* Lexington, Kentucky, University Press, 1975.

O'Dea, Janet K., Thomas F. O'Dea, and Charles J. Adams, ed. *Judaism, Christianity and Islam.* New York, Harper & Row Publishers, 1972.

Otto, Rudolf. *The Idea of the Holy.* London: Oxford University Press.

Paris, Peter J. *The Social Teaching of the Black Churches.* Philadelphia, PA: Fortress Press, 1985.

Payne, Ernest A. *Fellowship of Believers: Baptist Thought and Practice.* Southampton Row, London, Kingsgate Press, 1944.

Proctor, Samuel DeWitt. *The Substance of Things Hoped For: A Memoir of African-American Faith.* Valley Forge, PA: Judson Press, 1995.

Raboteau, Albert J. *Canaan Land: A Religious History of African Americans.* New York, Oxford University Press, 2001.

Russell, Malik. "FBI Reports Increase in Hate Crimes Against African Americans," The Crisis, Jan/Feb 2005, http://www.findarticles.com/p/articles/mi_qa4081/is_ai_n9522077 (Jan/Feb 2005).

Schlafly, Phyllis. "George Washington's Advise," Eagle Forum *http://www.usiap.org/Legacy/Quotes?George Washington.html* (13 July 2006).

Schaller, Lyle E. *The Very Large Church: New Rules for Leaders.* Nashville, Tennessee, Abingdon Press, 2000.

Schreiter, Robert R. *Constructing Local Theologies* (Mary Knoll, NY: Orbis, 1986.

Segler, Franklin M. *Christian Worship: It's Theology and Practice.* Nashville, Tennessee, Broadman Press, 1967.

Stallings, George A. "Renegade Priest," Emerge Magazine, Volume 6 (April 1995,): 22, 23.

Steele, Shelby. *The Content of our Character: A New Vision of Race in America.* New York, NY: Harper Perennial/Harper Collins Publishers, 1990.

Steinhorn, Leonard and Barbara Diggs –Brown. *By The Color of our Skin: The Illusion of Integration and the Reality of Race.* New York, A Plume Book, 1999.

Tippit, Sammy. *The Choice: America at the Crossroads of Ruin and Revival.* Chicago, Moody Press, 1998.

Tillich, Paul. *Theology of Culture.* London, Oxford University Press, 1970.

Trobisch Walter, "God's World Strategy" (Evangelize Magazine, 1957).

Warren, Rick. *The Purpose Driven Church.* Grand Rapids, MI: Zondervan Publishing House, 1995.

Webber, Robert E. *Ancient-Future Faith: Rethinking Evangelism for a Postmodern World.* Grand Rapids, Michigan Baker Books, 2004.

White, James F. *Protestant Worship: Traditions in Transition.* Louisville, Kentucky, Westminster/John Knox Press, 1985.

Woodson, Carter G. *The History of the Negro Church.* Washington, D.C. The Associated Publishers, Association for the Study of Negro Life and History, 1921.

Index

CPSIA information can be obtained at www.ICGtesting.com
Printed in the USA
LVOW08s2116070414

380689LV00001B/18/P